BRIGHT NOTES

A MIDSUMMER NIGHT'S DREAM BY WILLIAM SHAKESPEARE

Intelligent Education

Nashville, Tennessee

BRIGHT NOTES: A Midsummer Night's Dream
www.BrightNotes.com

No part of this publication may be used or reproduced in any manner whatsoever without written permission, except in the case of brief quotations in critical articles and reviews. For permissions, contact Influence Publishers http://www.influencepublishers.com.

ISBN: 978-1-645425-48-9 (Paperback)
ISBN: 978-1-645425-49-6 (eBook)

Published in accordance with the U.S. Copyright Office Orphan Works and Mass Digitization report of the register of copyrights, June 2015.

Originally published by Monarch Press.
Eve Leoff, 1964
2020 Edition published by Influence Publishers.

Interior design by Lapiz Digital Services. Cover Design by Thinkpen Designs.

Printed in the United States of America.

Library of Congress Cataloging-in-Publication Data forthcoming.
Names: Intelligent Education
Title: BRIGHT NOTES: A Midsummer Night's Dream
Subject: STU004000 STUDY AIDS / Book Notes

CONTENTS

1) Introduction to William Shakespeare — 1

2) Introduction to A Midsummer Night's Dream — 12

3) Textual Analysis
   - Act 1 — 18
   - Act 2 — 33
   - Act 3 — 56
   - Act 4 — 81
   - Act 5 — 92

4) Character Analyses — 99

5) Critical Commentary — 110

6) Essay Questions and Answers — 117

7) Bibliography — 124

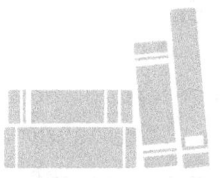

INTRODUCTION TO WILLIAM SHAKESPEARE

FACTS VERSUS SPECULATION

Anyone who wishes to know where documented truth ends and where speculation begins in Shakespearean scholarship and criticism first needs to know the facts of Shakespeare's life. A medley of life records suggest, by their lack of inwardness, how little is known of Shakespeare's ideology, his beliefs and opinions.

William Shakespeare was baptized on April 26, 1564, as "Gulielmus filius Johannes Shakespeare"; the evidence is the parish register of Holy Trinity Church, Stratford, England.

HUSBAND AND FATHER

On November 28, 1582, the Bishop of Worcester issued a license to William Shakespeare and "Anne Hathaway of Stratford" to solemnize a marriage upon one asking of the banns providing that there were no legal impediments. Three askings of the banns were (and are) usual in the Church of England.

On May 26, 1583, the records of the parish church in Stratford note the baptism of Susanna, daughter to William Shakespeare. The inference is clear, then, that Anne Hathaway Shakespeare was with child at the time of her wedding.

On February 2, 1585, the records of the parish church in Stratford note the baptisms of "Hamnet & Judith, son and daughter to William Shakespeare."

SHAKESPEARE INSULTED

On September 20, 1592, Robert Greene's A Groats-worth of witte, bought with a million of Repentance was entered in the Stationers' Register. In this work Shakespeare was publicly insulted as "an upstart Crow, beautified with our ["gentlemen" playwrights usually identified as Marlowe, Nashe, and Lodge] feathers, that with Tygers hart wrapt in a Players hyde [a **parody** of a Shakespearean line in II Henry VI] supposes he is as well able to bombast out a **blank verse** as the best of you: and being an absolute Johannes factotum, is in his own conceit the only Shake-scene in a country." This statement asperses not only Shakespeare's art but intimates his base, i.e., non-gentle, birth. A "John factotum" is a servant or a man of all work.

On April 18, 1593, Shakespeare's long erotic poem Venus and Adonis was entered for publication. It was printed under the author's name and was dedicated to the nineteen-year-old Henry Wriothesley, Earl of Southampton.

On May 9, 1594, another long erotic poem, *The Rape of Lucrece*, was entered for publication. It also was printed under Shakespeare's name and was dedicated to the Earl of Southampton.

On December 26 and 27, 1594, payment was made to Shakespeare and others for performances at court by the Lord Chamberlain's servants.

For August 11, 1596, the parish register of Holy Trinity Church records the burial of "Hamnet filius William Shakespeare."

FROM "VILLEIN" TO "GENTLEMAN"

On October 20, 1596, John Shakespeare, the poet's father, was made a "gentleman" by being granted the privilege of bearing a coat of arms. Thus, William Shakespeare on this day also became a "gentleman." Shakespeare's mother, Mary Arden Shakespeare, was "gentle" by birth. The poet was a product of a cross-class marriage. Both the father and the son were technically "villeins" or "villains" until this day.

On May 24, 1597, William Shakespeare purchased New Place, a large house in the center of Stratford.

CITED AS "BEST"

In 1598 Francis Meres's Palladis Tamia listed Shakespeare more frequently than any other English author. Shakespeare was cited as one of eight by whom "the English tongue is mightily enriched, and gorgeouslie invested in rare ornaments and resplendent abiliments"; as one of six who had raised monumentum aere perennius [a monument more lasting than brass]; as one of five who excelled in lyric poetry; as one of thirteen "best for Tragedie," and as one of seventeen who were "best for Comedy."

On September 20, 1598, Shakespeare is said on the authority of Ben Jonson (in his collection of plays, 1616) to have been an actor in Jonson's *Every Man in His Humour*.

On September 8, 1601, the parish register of Holy Trinity in Stratford records the burial of "Mr. Johannes Shakespeare," the poet's father.

BECOMES A "KING'S MAN"

In 1603 Shakespeare was named among others, the Lord Chamberlain's players, as licensed by James I (Queen Elizabeth having died) to become the King's Men.

In 1603 a garbled and pirated Hamlet (now known as Q1) was printed with Shakespeare's name on the title page.

In March 1604, King James gave Shakespeare, as one of the Grooms of the Chamber (by virtue of being one of the King's Men), four yards of red cloth for a livery, this being in connection with a royal progress through the City of London.

In 1604 (probably) there appeared a second version of *Hamlet* (now known as Q2), enlarged and corrected, with Shakespeare's name on the title page.

On June 5, 1607, the parish register at Stratford records the marriage of "M. John Hall gentleman & Susanna Shakespeare," the poet's elder daughter. John Hall was a doctor of medicine.

BECOMES A GRANDFATHER

On February 21, 1608, the parish register at Holy Trinity, Stratford, records the baptism of Elizabeth Hall, Shakespeare's first grandchild.

On September 9, 1608, the parish register at Holy Trinity, Stratford, records the burial of Mary Shakespeare, the poet's mother.

On May 20, 1609, "Shakespeare's Sonnets. Never before Imprinted" was entered for publication.

On February 10, 1616, the marriage of Judith, Shakespeare's younger daughter, is recorded in the parish register of Holy Trinity, Stratford.

On March 25, 1616, Shakespeare made his will. It is extant.

On April 23, 1616, Shakespeare died. The monument in the Stratford church is authority for the date.

BURIED IN STRATFORD CHURCH

On April 25, 1616, Shakespeare was buried in Holy Trinity Church, Stratford. Evidence of this date is found in the church register. A stone laid over his grave bears the inscription:

Good Frend for Jesus Sake Forbeare, To Digg The Dust Encloased Heare! Bleste Be Ye Man Yt Spares Thes Stones, And Curst Be He Yt Moves My Bones.

DEMAND FOR MORE INFORMATION

These are the life records of Shakespeare. Biographers, intent on book length or even short accounts of the life of the poet, of necessity flesh out these (and other) not very revealing notices from 1564-1616, Shakespeare's life span with ancillary matter such as the status of Elizabethan actors, details of the Elizabethan theaters, and life under Elizabeth I and James I. Information about Shakespeare's artistic life-for example, his alteration of his sources-is much more abundant than truthful insights into his personal life, including his beliefs. There is, of course, great demand for colorful stories about Shakespeare, and there is intense pressure on biographers to depict the poet as a paragon of wisdom.

ANECDOTES-TRUE OR UNTRUE?

Biographers of Shakespeare may include stories about Shakespeare that have been circulating since at least the seventeenth century; no one knows whether or not these stories are true. One declares that Shakespeare was an apprentice to a butcher, that he ran away from his master, and was received by actors in London. Another story holds that Shakespeare was, in his youth, a schoolmaster somewhere in the country. Another story has Shakespeare fleeing from his native town to escape the clutches of Sir Thomas Lucy who had often had him whipped and sometimes imprisoned for poaching deer. Yet another story represents the youthful Shakespeare as holding horses and taking care of them while their owners attended the theater. And there are other stories.

Scholarly and certainly lay expectations oblige Shakespearean biographers often to resort to speculation. This may be very well if biographers use such words as conjecture, presumably, seems, and almost certainly. I quote an example of this kind of hedged thought and language from Hazelton Spencer's *The Art and Life of William Shakespeare* (1940); "Of politics Shakespeare seems to have steered clear ... but at least by implication Shakespeare reportedly endorses the strong-monarchy policy of the Tudors and Stuarts." Or one may say, as I do in my book *Blood Will Tell in Shakespeare's Plays* (1984): "Shakespeare particularly faults his numerous villeins for lacking the classical virtue of courage (they are cowards) and for deficiencies in reasoning ability (they are 'fools'), and in speech (they commit malapropisms), for lack of charity, for ambition, for unsightly faces and poor physiques, for their smell, and for their harboring lice." This remark is not necessarily biographical or reflective of Shakespeare's personal beliefs; it refers to Shakespeare's art in that it makes general assertions about the base - those who lacked coats of arms-as they appear in the poet's thirty-seven plays. The remark's truth or lack of truth may be tested by examination of Shakespeare's writings.

WHO WROTE SHAKESPEARE'S PLAYS?

The less reputable biographers of Shakespeare, including some of weighty names, state assumptions as if they were facts concerning the poet's beliefs. Perhaps the most egregious are those who cannot conceive that the Shakespearean plays were written by a person not a graduate of Oxford or Cambridge and destitute of the insights permitted by foreign travel and by life at court. Those of this persuasion insist that the seventeenth Earl of Oxford, Edward de Vere (whose descendant Charles Vere recently spoke up for the Earl's authorship of the Shakespearean plays), or Sir Francis Bacon, or someone else wrote the Shakespearean plays. It is also argued that the stigma of publication would besmirch the honor of an Elizabethan gentleman who published under his own name (unless he could pretend to correct a pirated printing of his writings).

BEN JONSON KNEW HIM WELL

Suffice it here to say that the thought of anyone writing the plays and giving them to the world in the name of Shakespeare would have astonished Ben Jonson, a friend of the poet, who literally praised Shakespeare to the skies for his comedies and tragedies in the fine poem "To the Memory of My Beloved Master the Author, Mr. William Shakespeare, and What He Hath Left Us" (printed in the *First Folio*, 1623). Much more commonplace and therefore much more obtrusive upon the minds of Shakespeare students are those many scholars who are capable of writing, for example, that Shakespeare put more of himself into Hamlet than any of his other characters or that the poet had no rigid system of religion or morality. Even George Lyman Kittredge, the greatest American Shakespearean, wrote, "Hamlet's advice to the players has always been understood - and rightly - to embody Shakespeare's own views on the art of acting."

In point of fact, we know nothing of Shakespeare's beliefs or opinions except such obvious inferences as that he must have thought New Place, Stratford, worth buying because he bought it. Even Homer, a very self-effacing poet, differs in this matter from Shakespeare. Twice in the *Iliad* he speaks in his own voice (distinguished from the dialogue of his characters) about certain evil deeds of Achilles. Shakespeare left no letters, no diary, and no prefaces (not counting conventionally obsequious dedications); no Elizabethan Boswell tagged Shakespeare around London and the provinces to record his conversation and thus to reveal his mind. In his plays Shakespeare employed no raisonneur, or authorial mouthpiece, as some other dramatists have done: contrary to many scholarly assertions, it cannot be proved that Prospero, in *The Tempest* in the speech ending "I'll drown my book" (Act V), and Ulysses, in *Troilus and Cressida* in the long speech on "degree" (Act II), speak Shakespeare's own sentiments. All characters in all Shakespearean plays speak for themselves. Whether they speak also for Shakespeare cannot be proved because documents outside the plays cannot be produced.

As for the sonnets, they have long been the happy hunting ground of biographical crackpots who lack outside documents, who do not recognize that Shakespeare may have been using a persona, and who seem not to know that in Shakespeare's time good **sonnets** were supposed to read like confessions.

Some critics even go to the length of professing to hear Shakespeare speaking in the speech of a character and uttering his private beliefs. An example may be found in A. L. Rowse's *What Shakespeare Read and Thought* (1981): "Nor is it so difficult to know what Shakespeare thought or felt. A writer, Logan Pearsall Smith, had the perception to see that a personal tone of voice enters when Shakespeare is telling you what he thinks, sometimes almost a raised voice; it is more obvious again when he urges the same point over and over."

BUT THERE'S NO PROOF!

Rowse, deeply enamoured of his ability to hear Shakespeare's own thoughts in the speeches of characters speaking in character, published a volume entitled Shakespeare's *Self-Portrait, Passages from His Work* (1984). One critic might hear Shakespeare voicing his own thoughts in a speech in Hamlet; another might hear the author in *Macbeth*. Shakespearean writings can become a vast whispering gallery where Shakespeare himself is heard hic et ubique (here and everywhere), without an atom of documentary proof.

"BETTER SO"

Closer to truth is Matthew Arnold's poem on Shakespeare:

Others abide our question. Thou art free. We ask and ask - thou smilest and art still, Out-topping knowledge. For the loftiest hill, Who to the stars uncrowns his majesty, Planting his steadfast footsteps in the sea, Making the heaven of heavens his dwelling Spares but the cloudy border of his base To the foiled searching of mortality; And thou, who didst the stars and sunbeams know, Self-schooled, self-scanned, self-honored, self-secure, Didst tread the earth unguessed at. - Better so....

Here Arnold has Dichtung und Wahrheit - both poetry and truth - with at least two abatements: he exaggerates Shakespeare's wisdom - the poet, after all, is not God; and Arnold fails to acknowledge that Shakespeare's genius was variously recognized in his own time. Jonson, for example, recorded that the "players [actors of the poet's time] have often mentioned it as an honor to Shakespeare, that in his writing (whatsoever he penned) he never blotted a line" (*Timber*), and of course there is praise of Shakespeare, some of it quoted above, in Meres's *Palladis Tamia* (1598).

THE BEST APPROACH

Hippocrates' first apothegm states, "Art is long, but life is short." Even Solomon complained of too many books. One must be, certainly in our time, very selective. Shakespeare's ipsissima verba (his very words) should of course be studied, and some of them memorized. Then, if one has time, the golden insights of criticism from the eighteenth century to the present should be perused. (The problem is to find them all in one book!) And the vast repetitiousness, the jejune stating of the obvious, and the rampant subjectivity of much Shakespearean criticism should be shunned.

Then, if time serves, the primary sources of Shakespeare's era should be studied because the plays were not impervious to colorings imparted by the historical matrix. Finally, if the exigencies of life permit, biographers of Shakespeare who distinguish between fact and guesswork, such as Marchette Chute (*Shakespeare of London*), should be consulted. The happiest situation, pointed to by Jesus in Milton's *Paradise Regained*, is to bring judgment informed by knowledge to whatever one reads.

A MIDSUMMER NIGHT'S DREAM

INTRODUCTION

SHAKESPEARE AND A MIDSUMMER NIGHT'S DREAM: THE SOURCES

The probable sources of this play are Chaucer and Plutarch for Theseus, Huon of Bordeaux for Oberon, and *The Discovery of Witchcraft* by Reginald Scot for the character of Robin Goodfellow, and also for the incident of a man changed into an ass. Apuleius' *Golden Ass* is a possible source for the latter incident also. In addition, there is an analogous transformation in *Thesaurus Linguae Romanae et Britannicae*, where an ass's head is put on Midas. For the *Pyramus and Thisbe* material, the probable source is Ovid, translated by Golding. J. Thomson's *A Handful of Pleasant Delites* may also be a source for the latter material. Analogous material on *Pyramus and Thisbe* may be found in the above-mentioned Thesaurus. Greene's *James IV*, Lyly's *Endymion*, Marlowe's *Dido*, and Montemayor's *Diana* have been introduced into the source studies by scholars because of hints and echoes of *A Midsummer Night's Dream*.

THE OCCASION OF A MIDSUMMER NIGHT'S DREAM

Because the play is concerned so centrally with marriages and a royal wedding, it is thought that Shakespeare wrote *A Midsummer Night's Dream* to celebrate some wedding between two noble persons. The following weddings have been suggested: (1) Robert, Earl of Essex and Frances, Lady Sidney in April or May, 1590; (2) Sir Thomas Heneage and Mary, Countess of Southampton, on 2 May 1594; (3) William Stanley, Earl of Derby, and Elizabeth Vere at Greenwich on 26 January 1595; (4) Thomas Berkeley and Elizabeth Carey at Blackfriars on 19 February 1596; (5) Henry, Earl of Southampton, and Elizabeth Vernon about February or August, 1598; (6) Henry, Lord Herbert, and Anne Russell at Blackfriars on 16 June, 1600. The most likely are (3) and (4), because (1), (2), and (5) brought disfavor from the Queen and it is thought that she attended whatever wedding this play was performed at, which she would not have done if she disapproved of the match. She was at (3), (6), and probably (4), but (6) is ruled out because the date is so late. For this latter reason, (1) and (5) are also ruled out. Therefore the effective choice is between (3) and (4), the Derby-Vere wedding in 1595 and the Berkeley-Carey wedding in 1596.

THE DATE OF A MIDSUMMER NIGHT'S DREAM

The wedding for which this play was performed is a factor in determining the date when it was written. The style of the play indicates that it belongs to the lyric group of 1594-1596. The bad weather referred to by Titania's speech in Scene 1 of Act 2 occurred in March, 1594, so the play must have been written after that time. Also, the mention of a lion frightening the ladies may refer to such an incident at the baptism of the Scottish Prince Henry on August 30, 1594. This indicates January, 1595, as the date of composition (the Derby-Vere wedding). If, however, "Pyramus and Thisbe" is a **parody** on *Romeo and Juliet*, then *A Midsummer Night's Dream* must be placed later than *Romeo and Juliet*, which would put the comedy in February, 1596 (the Berkeley-Carey wedding). For these reasons, the most likely date of composition is thought to be the winter of 1595-96. There are theories that the play underwent revisions extending over a number of years during the 1590s. The most extreme position is taken by John Dover Wilson in the New Cambridge edition of the play.

This noted critic says the original writing was in 1592 or earlier, with an intermediate revision in 1594, possibly for a wedding in both cases. Then he posits a final revision in 1598 for the Southampton wedding, covering the fairy scenes as well as the last act. Dover-Wilson rests his case on the differences in style within the play and on variations in the way characters are named in stage directions and speech prefixes. Sir E. K. Chambers thinks the differences in style are dictated by the subject matter involved, which is certainly incontestable. Chambers thinks variations in names can't be theorized upon - Shakespeare may just have been more relaxed about the matter at some times in a day's work. This seems a more likely explanation of such variations. Miss Edith Rickert suggests that this play was a political satire planned by Hertford in 1595 and then revised for public performance in 1598. Chambers seems correct in calling this theory incredible though ingenious.

BRIEF SUMMARY OF THE PLAY

The play opens in the palace of Theseus, Duke of Athens. Theseus is a mythical Greek hero. He is about to marry Hippolyta, Queen of the Amazons, a mythical race of women-warriors. Hermia's father, Egeus, comes before the Duke to ask that she be punished by law for disobeying him. Hermia wants to marry Lysander and Egeus wants her to marry Demetrius. The law he asks to be invoked provides that she die or enter a nunnery if she doesn't obey her father. We learn that Demetrius, her father's choice, has abandoned Helena. Helena still loves her unfaithful Demetrius. Lysander and Hermia plan to elope. They tell Helena, who says she'll tell Demetrius. All four lovers will go to the woods the next night: Hermia and Lysander to elope; Demetrius to prevent this, having been warned by Helena; and Helena herself to be with Demetrius. Thus, at this point a situation that was all right before the play began is now off balance, with the two men loving Hermia, and Helena sad and lovelorn.

In the next scene we are introduced to an entirely different group of characters. A number of Athenian workmen - Quince, Bottom, Flute, Snout, Snug, and Starveling - have come together to prepare a play as entertainment after the Duke's wedding. Their play is "Pyramus and Thisbe," a traditional tale of tragic love. Young lovers are separated by the animosity of their parents and through an error they kill themselves. These simple workmen are comically inept in their theatrical venture. One of their company, Bottom the weaver, is remarkable for his enthusiasm and self-confidence. He wants to play all the parts and gives examples of his ability. These characters agree to meet in the woods the next night to rehearse their play.

Next we enter another entirely different world. We are now in the wood mentioned in both at the previous scenes, and we meet Puck, or Robin Goodfellow, a mischievous spirit known for household pranks and rustic devilment. He is the helpmate of Oberon, King of the Fairies, whom we also meet here. We witness a quarrel between the King and his Queen, Titania. The Queen has a changeling that the King wants and she will not give him the boy. To get what he wants, Oberon plans to enchant the Queen's eyes with a love-juice that will cause her to fall madly in love with anyone or anything she sees. While she's thus diverted, he'll get the changeling. Oberon sends Puck to obtain the flower possessing this magic juice. The King witnesses Helena's one-sided love for Demetrius and when Puck returns he is instructed to apply the juice to Demetrius so that he'll love Helena.

The plot begins to thicken, for Puck anoints the eyelids of Lysander, who wakes and loves Helena. Helena has been deserted by Demetrius and when Lysander suddenly declares that he loves her she feels abused and leaves to continue looking for Demetrius. Lysander follows her, leaving Hermia asleep. Hermia wakes after he is gone and goes to look for him. The situation has been made worse, for now neither man loves the woman who loves him: Hermia loves Lysander, but Lysander loves Helena; Helena loves Demetrius, but Demetrius loves Hermia.

Titania has been enchanted by Oberon and awaits being awakened by her "beloved." Having seen our first group, the lovers, it is time to pick up our second group, the workmen. Therefore we now are with Bottom and his companions and they are rehearsing in the wood very near Titania's sleeping-place. Puck chances on the scene and he puts an ass's head on Bottom. The other workmen flee in fright and Bottom sings to show his courage, even though he's quite frightened himself, not knowing why they've run away. Titania is awakened by Bottom's song and she loves him, ass's head and all.

Hermia and Demetrius meet in the wood and by witnessing their conversation, Oberon sees that Puck has enchanted the wrong Athenian. In order to remedy the situation, he'll charm Demetrius. Now Helena and Lysander meet Demetrius, so events are at the height of confusion because both men claim to love Helena. This is the reverse of the beginning, when neither loved her. Hermia has been seeking Lysander. When she finds him, she finds also that he no longer loves her. All she can come up with in the way of an explanation is that Helena has stolen Lysander away by comparing her height to Hermia's small stature. Helena thinks the three others have banded together to make fun of her. The two girls quarrel. Finally Oberon has Puck apply a curative to Lysander so that he'll love Hermia again. Demetrius remains enchanted so that he'll love Helena.

Puck has told Oberon how Titania has fallen in love with the transformed Bottom. The King gets his changeling and then takes the charm off Titania. The lovers are awakened by Theseus, Hippolyta and Egeus. They can't say how it came about, but everything is finally right. The Duke declares that they'll have a triple wedding. Last to awaken is Bottom, who rightly declares the unfathomability of his "dream" and feels most profoundly its power. When he returns to his fellow workmen, we see their mutual affection and concern. We learn that their play of "Pyramus and Thisbe" is to be performed at court.

Finally, the wedding of Theseus and Hippolyta mentioned at the very beginning of the play takes place. Hermia and Lysander, Helena and Demetrius are married also. The workmen present their play amid much comment from the males present. After the household is asleep, the fairies enter and bless everything with peace and prosperity. Puck's last words to us suggest that the whole thing may be only a dream, and thus concludes *A Midsummer Night's Dream*.

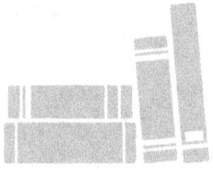

A MIDSUMMER NIGHT'S DREAM

TEXTUAL ANALYSIS

ACT 1

ACT 1: SCENE 1

The play opens in the palace of Theseus, Duke of Athens, a legendary Greek hero. He enters accompanied by his bride-to-be Hippolyta, queen of the Amazons. Theseus tells Hippolyta that although their wedding is only four days away, his impatience makes the time seem long. She answers that the interval will pass quickly. Both measure time by the moon - it is waning now and will be a new crescent on the night of their marriage. Theseus sends Philostrate, who is in charge of entertainment at the court, into the city to organize the public celebration of the wedding, and contrasts this planned merriment with his conquering Hippolyta initially in his war on the Amazons.

Comment

The play's **theme** of love and marriage is announced strongly and immediately by the opening exchange of speeches between

Theseus and Hippolyta (pronounced Hip-pol-i-ta). The repeated mention of the moon is important to note here, for it is mentioned often throughout the play. Shakespeare learned of Theseus from North's translation of Plutarch's *Lives of the Noble Grecians and Romans.* To Shakespeare and his contemporaries, Theseus was not legend but historical fact. Shakespeare also knew of Theseus from Chaucer's *Knight's Tale.* One of Theseus' legendary heroic exploits was his successful war on the Amazons, a mythical nation of women-warriors. Hippolyta's comment on how quickly time will pass is noteworthy because we shall see that indeed time does strange things when love is governing events.

Egeus, father of Hermia, comes before the Duke to complain about his daughter. He explains that while Demetrius has his consent to marry her, she has been "bewitched" by Lysander and wants to marry him, thus being disobedient. Accordingly Egeus asks that the law be enforced which provides for either her obedience or her death. Theseus questions Hermia, advising her that her father's authority over her is absolute and likening the relationship between father and daughter to that between a mold and wax. In reply to Theseus' declaration that Demetrius is worthy, she says that Lysander is, too. Theseus says that her father's approval makes Demetrius worthier, whereupon she counters with the wish that her father saw with her eyes. Theseus replies that her eyes must rather be governed by her father's judgment. She asks what may happen to her if she refuses to wed Demetrius. The Duke replies that she must die or become a nun, "chanting faint hymns to the cold, fruitless moon."

She must consider well whether she can undergo a life which, unlike a "rose distilled," rather withers "on the virgin thorn" and "grows, lives and dies in single blessedness." Hermia avows she would rather do thus than marry Demetrius because her father commands it. Theseus says she should think it over and announce her decision on the night of his marriage to Hippolyta. Demetrius and Lysander now exchange sharp words and, in presenting his case, Lysander reveals that there is a further complication. Demetrius has been false to Helena, who is still in love with him even though he has forsaken her by switching his affection to Hermia. Theseus says he's heard of this and he leaves with Hippolyta, taking Demetrius and Egeus with him. Lysander and Hermia are thus left alone on the stage to comment on their situation and plan what to do about it.

Comment

With the entrance of Egeus, the threads of the plot begin to emerge. The typical disgruntled father, he straight away announces this: "Full of vexation come I." His description of how Lysander has won Hermia away from proper obedience to her father's wishes is the classic view of the older, stolid generation toward young and wayward romance. Balconies by moonlight, love poetry, souvenirs, gifts of jewelry, flowers, and candy are all a silly nuisance. These interfere with the orderly, business-like fulfillment by a dutiful daughter of a marriage contract made by a responsible father. Thus the play's treatment of the **theme** of love and marriage is given the added dimension of Egeus' unfavorable view of courtship here, and the harsh penalty he asks be imposed against the kind of romance he decries will serve to advance the plot when Hermia and Lysander try to escape this penalty. The use of one's eyes in love is introduced here. We shall see that how well one "sees" where love is concerned is a crucial question in the play, and that linking judgment to vision is not as easy as Theseus would imply. The description of the relationship between Egeus and Hermia as similar to that between a mold and wax was frequently applied in Shakespeare's time to the parent-child relationship and also to the authority of men over women, whose minds were considered particularly impressionable and susceptible to the stronger male influence.

Theseus' speech on "single blessedness" mentions the moon and uses a rose in its famous characterization of single and married life, both references being in keeping with the play's special mood and atmosphere. Shakespeare uses similarly the idea of a flower distilled into perfume in a **sonnet** where he is speaking of how men may perpetuate themselves by having children. Though both Lysander and Demetrius love Hermia now, we learn here that Demetrius loved another girl, Helena, previously, and that she still loves him. Hermia does not want Demetrius, but Helena does. No one wants Helena, while both men claim Hermia. The pairs of lovers can be associated properly by noticing that the names Helena and Demetrius have an "e" as 2nd and 4th letter. They were once in love mutually and if Demetrius were still so, the other pair, whose love is mutual - Hermia and Lysander - would have no trouble.

Left alone, Hermia and Lysander discuss their situation, and Lysander remarks, "the course of true love never did run smooth." He suggests that they solve their problem by eloping the next night. He will meet Hermia in the woods outside of town and take her to his aunt's house, which is seven leagues away. A league is usually estimated at roughly three miles nowadays. There, free of Athenian law, they may marry. Hermia agrees, swearing "by all the vows that ever men have broke" that she will keep the appointment.

Comment

Although this thwarted love between Hermia and Lysander contains the ingredients of tragedy, we see here that the treatment is decidedly in a lighter, comic vein. Rather than a display of great passion and emotional strife, the foregoing speeches are so stylized and formal that what we observe are the typical young lovers in the typical thwarted romance. We are meant to respond to this and are kept from feeling the deeper, stronger, more tragic emotions which are potentially present. A league is a very indefinite measure, and combined with the fairy-tale number seven, the distance becomes a story-book journey through the woods to auntie's house. The measurement of distance, like that of time pointed out earlier, is adjusted to suit the play's own world, a world at whose center is a dream. Two obvious examples of the stylized formality noted in the lover's comments above are first, a type of dramatic dialogue called stichomythia, where characters speak single alternating lines (lines 136-140). It is worth noticing here because it is an extremely formal device, occurring very rarely in Shakespeare, but present again in this play and noted as such below. Secondly, the smoothness of the famous platitude about the course of true love not being smooth is a give-away to the emotional content here - it's a little too pat for a man really in the throes of deep suffering. It is interesting to note also that Hermia swears by the vows that men have broken. We shall see that in this play the men are inconstant in a comical degree.

Helena, Demetrius's forsaken but still doting girlfriend, now comes upon the scene. When Hermia addresses her as "fair Helena," her immediate reaction is to tell of her unhappy love for Demetrius. Helena says she herself is not fair since Demetrius loves Hermia's beauty. She wishes appearance were contagious the way sickness is so that she might be just like Hermia and so win back Demetrius.

> Comment

Hermia and Helena hear speak in alternating single lines of dialogue (lines 194-201), another case of stichomythia as explained above and again achieving an extremely formal, stiff effect. The sing-song of the contrast between the way Demetrius treats each girl takes the bite out of Helena's sad situation, and prevents us from taking it seriously.

To comfort Helena, Hermia and Lysander tell her about their plan to meet the next night in the woods by moonlight and elope. After they leave, Helena speaks her mind. She says love has transforming power. Cupid is a blind and winged boy because love does not see with the eyes but with the mind, does not involve the judgment, and is often perjured.

> Comment

In the theatre of Shakespeare, a character often thinks out loud this way and by this means, called a soliloquy, we in the audience know his mind. Helena's reference to transformation should be noted here. She also mentioned it when she wished she might catch Hermia's appearance like one does a sickness. Transformation is a very important **theme** in the play, and will be dealt with more fully as it reappears throughout. The relation of love to eyesight and vision is connected to the idea of transformation. We should note that Helena's mention of eyes and judgment here recalls the exchange on the subject noted earlier between Theseus and Hermia. Eyesight and judgment, vision and transformation are questions of first importance in this play. Helena's mentioning perjury in love echoes Hermia's swearing to meet Lysander, by all the vows that men have broken.

Now Helena refers to Demetrius' inconstancy and resolves to tell him of the planned elopement, betraying her friend so that she may win Demetrius' gratitude and, more important, follow him to the woods and thereby have his company.

SUMMARY

In this scene we learn the following:

(1) Theseus and Hippolyta are to be married.

(2) Hermia and Lysander want to be married, but

(3) Egeus, Hermia's father, wants her to marry Demetrius.

(4) Demetrius is loved by Helena, whom he loved before his present attachment to Hermia.

(5) All four lovers will go to the woods the next night: Hermia and Lysander to elope; Demetrius to prevent this, having been warned by Helena; and Helena herself to be with Demetrius.

Thus, at this point a situation that was all right before the play opened with each couple mutually in love (Demetrius and Helena, Lysander and Hermia) is now off balance, with the two men loving Hermia, and Helena sad and lovelorn.

ACT 1: SCENE 2

This scene also takes place in Athens, but instead of at the Ducal Palace, we are now among working men. We are now introduced to the following Athenian tradesmen: Quince the Carpenter,

Snug the Joiner, Bottom the Weaver, Flute the Bellows-mender, Snout the Tinker, and Starveling the Tailor.

> Comment

The name of each tradesman is suited to the work he does in some way, but the association is subtle enough not to seem artificial: these are real people with real names. Snug suits a joiner, and Snout as a tinker mends kettles with spouts. A flute is a wind instrument and so is a bellows, and tailors are traditionally undernourished. Quince is the name of a carpenter's tool, and a "bottom" is another name for a spool of thread and therefore associated with a weaver. However, as William Hazlitt pointed out admiringly, the names of the tradesmen please us most because we feel that they are natural and that it is just luck that they characterize each trade so well. Bottom's name and occupation have a further significance which we shall note as the play progresses.

These amiable, simple men have come together to prepare a play to be performed at the wedding of Theseus and Hippolyta. Quince is in charge and he begins by asking if all are present. Bottom, who is the most energetic participator, advises that Quince announce the name of the play and then call each man's name. Their play is, "The most lamentable comedy and most cruel death of Pyramus and Thisbe."

> Comment

The story of Pyramus and Thisbe was a popular tale of tragic love available to the Elizabethan in many forms and very familiar to Shakespeare's public. It concerns the traditional situation of lovers whose parents are enemies. Their secret meeting one moonlit night results in death for both, in a manner similar to that of *Romeo and Juliet*. The man, mistakenly thinking his lady is dead, kills himself; she, finding him dead, kills herself also. This **theme** is obviously related to the situation that has begun to unfold in the first scene concerning young love and its conflict with parental authority.

Nick Bottom is the first name called, and Quince says he is to play Pyramus. Bottom asks, is Pyramus a lover or a tyrant? When he finds that Pyramus is a lover who kills himself for love, Bottom declares his fitness for the part, though his "chief humor" is to play a tyrant. He gives a vigorous example of his talent in the latter capacity, reciting a fiery speech impromptu.

Comment

When Bottom speaks of his "chief humor," he means his inclination by temperament for the role of tyrant. The people of Shakespeare's time believed that the human body was made up chiefly of four fluids or "humors": phlegm, blood, choler, and melancholy (also called black choler). A person's disposition and his temporary state of mind were determined according to the relative proportions of these fluids in his body; consequently a person was said to be phlegmatic, sanguine, choleric, or melancholy. We still use these words to describe temperaments, though we have long abandoned the physiological theory which gave rise to them. The chief humor of Bottom, as he sees himself, is choler. Bottom's claim to be able to perform well in "Ercles' vein, a tyrant's vein" is a reference to Hercules, which was a popular stock ranting role. Bottom himself best describes what "ranting" is: "a part to tear a cat in, to make all split." The speech he gives to display his talent for this kind of part does indeed "tear" and "split" with its grating **alliterations** and pouncing rhymes. The "Phibbus' car" mentioned in the speech means the chariot of Phoebus Apollo, the sun god. Hercules Furens by Seneca portrayed the stock ranting figure of Hercules, and the style of Bottom's speech here parodies early translations of Seneca. In addition, we know that there were two major styles of acting in the Elizabethan theatre, an artificial style and a more natural one. From references throughout Shakespeare we know that he approved of the more natural style, and that he thought the other style pompous and bombastic. Therefore, here Shakespeare may be parodying also the artificial style of acting, which was prone to become "ranting."

After Bottom is named to play Pyramus, Quince names Francis Flute the bellows-mender to play Thisbe. Flute asks if Thisbe is "a wandering knight." Quince answers that Thisbe is the lady that Pyramus loves. Flute objects to playing a woman, saying that he has a beard coming. Quince says that doesn't matter for he shall wear a mask and speak in a falsetto.

Comment

A wandering knight is a knight-errant, who, along with a lover and a tyrant, was a typical role of the time. All female parts were played by boy actors in the theatre of Shakespeare's day. There were no women actors at all. When we consider what magnificent women Shakespeare has created in his plays, we realize what excellent actors these boys must have been. It is hard to imagine a boy playing Juliet or Cleopatra, but that was the case in the days when Shakespeare's plays were first performed before an audience of his contemporaries.

Hearing that Thisbe will be played in a mask, Bottom says if he may wear a mask he would like to play Thisbe too. He says he will speak in a "monstrous little voice" and he gives an example of his prowess in this regard. Quince insists, however, that Bottom play Pyramus and Flute, Thisbe. Bottom is temporarily quieted and with an air of injured magnanimity he allows the casting to proceed. We shall see that he is only subdued for a moment. Quince then names Robin Starveling for Thisbe's mother, Tom Snout for Pyramus' father, and himself for Thisbe's father.

Comment

The parents of Pyramus and Thisbe are mentioned in the source story, but they do not appear in the play as acted. When the time comes for these tradesmen to perform, we shall see that Quince, Starveling, and Snout have new parts.

Finally, Quince names Snug the joiner for the lion's part. Snug inquires if Quince has the lion's part written out, because if so, Snug would like to begin studying it. He is "slow of study" and wants to be sure to know it on time. Quince assures him that he may do it extempore, for all he has to do is roar. When he hears this, the irrepressible Bottom can no longer contain himself. He has been quiet for all of eleven lines, but the prospect of roaring is too much for him. He must chime in again: "Let me play the lion too." He enthusiastically describes how well he would roar. It will do people good to hear him and the Duke will request an encore. Quince and the others agree that to roar "too terribly" might frighten the Duchess and the ladies, causing them to shriek, and they would all be hanged for it. Bottom won't be stopped. First, he has a joke on the subject - if the ladies are frightened out of their wits, then they may be so foolish (being witless) as to hang them. Second, he has the necessary modification all ready. He will roar as gently as a dove or a nightingale.

Comment

The lover and the tyrant whom Bottom could undertake equally well are the same kind of direct opposites as a dove and a nightingale on the one hand, which are birds of love, and a lion on the other hand, fierce and savage king of the beasts. Thus Bottom is ready to take on anything. He has complete confidence in his ability to sweep thus from one end of the emotional scale to the other. Bottom the weaver is one of Shakespeare's most extraordinary creations. The energy and enthusiasm with which he participates in life are immediately evident. Some critics have objected to what they consider his domineering, brash, self-centered personality, but this is a gross misunderstanding. His eagerness and vitality evince a love of life and a willingness to engage in it to his fullest capacity. Such a man cannot help but win our affection as we shall see he has won that of his comrades. We shall see that his talent for life, the beauty of his fresh, naive eagerness will win for him a special place in this play where love and art and dreams assert their power over life. Bottom, the fundamental realist his name implies, will feel the power they assert most profoundly. His glory will be that starting from his position as a rock-bottom realist he can, with the same vigor and joy he brings to whatever he does, respond to his power and believe. The energy of his love of life unifies experience, and he is a weaver in this deeper sense too, as shall be seen.

Despite the adroitness of Bottom's bid to play the Lion too, Quince insists he can play no part but Pyramus, persuasively citing as reasons that Pyramus is "sweet-faced," handsome ("proper"), and "a most lovely gentlemanlike man." Therefore, says the foxy Quince, Bottom has to play Pyramus. Bottom at long last deigns to accept only the one role, little enough for his talents albeit the best part in the play. Having watched his virtuoso performance in this scene, we must share his self-estimate. Once his part has been narrowed to one, Bottom immediately opens up possibilities within it. He asks Quince what color beard he ought to wear and when Quince leaves it up to him, Bottom recites with great relish all the possible colors in beards: "straw-color," "orange-tawny," "purple-in-grain" or "French-crown-color beard, your perfit yellow." Thus he has already embarked with gusto on his theatrical venture. Quince makes a joke on "French-crown-color" saying that some French crowns have no hair at all and then Bottom would be playing bare-faced. Quince hands out the scripts and tells his actors to learn them for a rehearsal the next night. They are to meet in the palace wood a mile outside of town by moonlight. There, Quince states, they will have the privacy and secrecy not possible if they were to meet in the city.

In the meantime, Quince will assemble the necessary properties. Bottom agrees to this on behalf of everybody, saying, "there we may rehearse most obscenely and courageously." His excitement at the prospect carries him away and he uses the wrong word. Quince specifies the meeting place as the Duke's Oak. Naturally it is Bottom who has the last words in the scene as with sporting verve but only hazy meaning he says, "Enough. Hold, or cut bowstrings." We gather the meaning by the energy of the words, but we can only guess at their precise definition.

Comment

It has been pointed out that Bottom's occupation as a weaver would make him particularly well-acquainted with various dyes. Also, costumes in the theatre of Shakespeare's time were extremely elaborate, and actors in general would be greatly concerned with their apparel for a part. By French-crown color, Bottom means the golden color of the French coin. The joke that Quince makes about this is because syphilis was called the French disease (every country blamed it on another - in France it was called the English disease), and he is saying that the heads ("crowns") of those with the French disease are bald. Bottom's use of words in the foregoing scene is comically inept, but through the sheer force of his personality he gets his meaning across. Perhaps he uses the word "obscenely" because it includes the word "scene" and he thinks it means something like putting forth a scene. His last words seem to be an archer's expression, probably meaning, "keep your promises or give up the play." A reference to archery is not out of keeping with this play. Hippolyta, who as an Amazon would be an excellent archer, describes the moon as a silver bow in scene one. Cupid's bow and arrow will be important later. Therefore Bottom's ineptitude manages somehow to be meaningful. Finally, it should be noted that this scene is in prose and is meant to contrast with the formal poetry of the lovers in scene one. Prose is often used in Shakespeare for characters who contribute realistic, down-to-earth comedy to a play.

SUMMARY

The following should be noted about the foregoing scene:

(1) We are introduced to characters who are very, very different from those we met in scene one. This difference is expressed markedly by their language. The characters in this scene speak in the prose of comic realism, which contrasts with the formal poetry the lovers speak.

(2) However, connections between these two distinctly different groups have been established in three important ways:

(a) The reason these men are preparing a play is to entertain at that same wedding of Theseus and Hippolyta discussed in Scene 1, at which Hermia must announce her decision.

(b) The subject of the play they have chosen, while comically distant from their own world, is relevant to Hermia's plight.

(c) Their plan to rehearse the next night in the Duke's wood a mile out of town by moonlight brings them into the same geographical area as the lovers who also plan to meet there. We can expect plot development from the physical proximity of these otherwise entirely, separate worlds. In other words, we should be alerted that Shakespeare has brought the two different groups into the same woods for some plot reason.

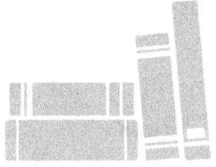

A MIDSUMMER NIGHT'S DREAM

TEXTUAL ANALYSIS

ACT 2

ACT 2: SCENE 1

This scene takes place in that wood near Athens which has been designated as a meeting place for the characters in each of the two preceding scenes. Puck or Robin Goodfellow and a Fairy enter from opposite sides. Puck inquires about the fairy's activities. The spirit answers in light and airy song, describing how he wanders everywhere more swiftly than the moon. He serves the Fairy Queen by taking care of the flowers which he calls her "pensioners" (members of the royal bodyguard in splendid uniforms). Specifically, he hangs dewdrops on the gold and ruby-spotted cowslips. The fairy bids farewell to Puck, saying the Queen and all her elves will come there soon. Puck says the King of the Fairies, Oberon, plans to be there also, and he warns the fairy to keep the Queen out of the King's sight, because King Oberon is very angry at his Queen. Queen Titania has a changeling, a lovely boy stolen from an Indian King, and Oberon is jealous and wants the child for his own. Titania not only withholds the changeling, but makes the little boy her special favorite. And so, Puck continues, every time Oberon and Titania meet, whether in wood or meadow, by a spring or under the stars, they quarrel so fiercely that all their elves are frightened and crawl into acorn cups to hide.

Comment

The fairies in *A Midsummer Night's Dream* are Shakespeare's invention. There had, of course, been fairies in English folklore, but Shakespeare's differ in several important respects from these. It is Shakespeare's fairies as depicted here which have held sway over the public imagination ever since, replacing those of folk tradition. Shakespeare's differ from the latter in three outstanding ways: their diminutive size, their association with flowers, and their benevolent natures. The fairy of folklore had none of these characteristics. The popular conception which has prevailed has them because it is derived from Shakespeare's creation in this play. The Fairy's song with which the scene opens introduces still another kind of language into the play. Like that of the lovers and of the workmen, it expresses a different kind of character. It comes into being because this particular character requires it. The variety of language in this play, suitable kind of character who speaks it and serving to differentiate between characters, is one of Shakespeare's triumphs. We note, of course, the mention once again of the moon and flowers.

After Puck's description of the frightened elves, so tiny that they can hide in acorn cups, the Fairy asks Puck if he is Robin Goodfellow. In asking the question, the Fairy describes some of the activities attributed to the elf Robin: frightening village maidens, skimming milk so it won't churn, taking the kick out of liquor, misleading people who travel at night, and for those who treat him well, doing work and bringing luck. Puck answers that he is the mischievous Robin Goodfellow, Hobgoblin, and Puck, and he recounts some more of his mischief. Besides being jester to King Oberon, he fools horses by neighing like a filly and he makes old women spill ale on themselves by getting into their cups in the shape of a "crab" and bobbing against their lips. Sometimes he pretends he's a three-foot stool and when a wise, old woman, in the middle of a sad tale, tries to sit down, he moves, she falls, crying "tailor" and coughing, and everybody laughs uproariously.

Comment

Puck is a general name for mischievous devils or imps but here is Robin Goodfellow, a household elf common in country folklore. The pranks Shakespeare credits him with here are homespun, domestic mischief, rich in colorful associations with English rural life. As well as doing all kinds of naughty tricks, Puck could be very helpful and do useful household tasks if so inclined. "Hobgoblin" means Robin the goblin, because "Hob" is a country form of Robert or Robin. A "crab" is a crab apple. The cry of the old woman, "tailor," means either one with a tail or refers to the fact that tailors sit on the floor.

Puck concludes his speech with the announcement that Oberon is approaching. The Fairy says so is his mistress, Titania, and he wishes Oberon were gone. At this point, the King of Fairies, Oberon, enters with his train at one door and the Queen, Titania, enters with her train at another. Oberon addresses Titania as "proud Titania" and calls their moonlight meeting unfortunate. She replies by calling him "jealous Oberon," and starts to leave, saying she has forsworn his bed and company. Oberon calls her a "rash wanton" (willful creature) and tells her to stay, reminding her that he is her lord. Titania replies that if he is her lord, she must be his lady. Then she begins reciting all his extracurricular romances as an ironical commentary on his claim to being her lord and master. She says he has stolen from fairyland and in the shape of the typical shepherd, Corin, he has played on pipes and sung love poetry to the shepherdess, Phillida. Titania continues by pointing out that he has come from faraway India only because Hippolyta is an old girlfriend who's getting married. The Queen's description of Hippolyta is finely sarcastic: "the bouncing Amazon,/Your buskined mistress and your warrior love." She closes by saying Oberon has come all that way to bless the marriage of Theseus and Hippolyta because he's sweet on the bride. Oberon immediately and indignantly rises in self-defense, saying Titania ought to be ashamed to bring that Hippolyta business up since he knows about her love for Theseus. Oberon then neatly rattles off the names of four women whom Theseus abandoned for Titania: the ravished Perigenia, Aegles, Ariadne, and Antiopa.

Comment

When the King and Queen of the Fairies enter, they immediately address each other by name, thus informing the audience of their identity. Their feelings about each other are also skillfully communicated right away by Oberon's addressing Titania as "proud," and by her responding with "jealous Oberon." We not only learn who these characters are by these modes of address, but we learn what each thinks of the other. Accomplished in less than two lines, this is great dramatic economy. In one more line we learn another important piece of information. The result of the quarrel between them is that Titania has foresworn Oberon's bed and company. So again, the course of love is not running smoothly, only here we have a new variation of the same theme.

The threat to Hermia is that she might have to foreswear what Titania chooses to give up here, while poor Helena has already had to do so against her will. In all three cases, love matters certainly need straightening out.

Corin and Phillida are typical names for a shepherd and shepherdess in pastoral poetry (poetry dealing with rural life). The pipes of corn she accuses him of playing on are pipes made of grain stalks, usually oats. Buskins are a kind of leather legging. Perigenia is the Perigouna of Plutarch's account, one of Theseus' several mistresses. Aegles is North's spelling of Aegle, another of Theseus' mistresses. Ariadne was the daughter of Minos of Crete. She helped Theseus thread the labyrinth to kill the Minotaur and was abandoned by him on the island of Naxos when he returned to Athens. Antiopa is another name for Hippolyta, the Amazonian queen conquered by Theseus.

Titania replies to this onslaught of her past amours with Theseus by accusing Oberon of making them up out of jealousy. She goes on to say that never, since the beginning of midsummer, has she been free of his brawling. Wherever they meet - hill, dale, forest, meadow, fountain, brook or seashore - he disturbs their merrymaking, as they dance with the wind in their hair. Therefore, she continues, since they piped music for the fairy dancing all in vain, the winds took revenge by sucking up contagious fogs from the sea and bringing them to land with disastrous results. These fogs have caused even "pelting" (paltry) rivers to overflow their banks. The resultant flooding has meant wasted labor for both the ox in the yoke and the ploughman driving him. The corn in these flooded fields has rotted while still green and immature. The pens where sheep and cattle should be, stand empty mid the general devastation, and the crows grow fat on the livestock dead of the murrain disease. The areas set aside for outdoor games, such as the nine men's morris (a game played on squares cut in the turf with counters such as pebbles or pegs), or the mazes, are filled with mud and indistinguishable from lack of use.

Titania continues that though men have all the hardships of that season, they have none of the comforts and compensations of winter, no hymns or carols bless the night. Because of Oberon's quarrel with her, says Titania, the moon, who is in control of floods, is pale with anger and keeps the whole atmosphere so drenched that "rheumatic diseases" (colds, grippe, rheumatism) are very prevalent. And as a result of the foregoing disorder in nature ("distemperature"), the seasons are all mixed up. Frosts kill new roses, buds follow fast upon wintry days, none of the seasons act the way they are supposed to. People, watching in amazement for the usual indications for each season don't know which is which. Titania concludes by repeating that this string of evil consequences can be traced directly to their quarrel as its cause and origin. They "are the parents and the original" of this evil offspring.

Comment

This famous passage about the weather is thought to be an **allusion** to the very bad weather of March, 1594, in England. This is significant because it is used as evidence for dating the play. If Titania is describing weather that prevailed in March, 1594, then *A Midsummer Night's Dream* must have been written after that date. Other information is used to ascertain a date before which it probably had to be written, so that scholars arrive at the date 1595-96 for the composition of this play.

We should note that marital discord is here made responsible for violent disorder in the natural world. So we are still on the subject of love problems. The recitation of old romances with which each upbraided the other also serves to remind us of the problems of Hermia and Helena. Even these superior beings, the King and Queen of Fairyland, whose quarrels change the order of the seasons, are subject to the same vagaries in love. And by their mention of dealings with Theseus and Hippolyta, these latter lofty personages are also seen to be not too high for love's ups and downs. Thus the Fairy Kingdom, though inhabited by very different creatures, has strong connections with the worlds we have already met. Not only does dissension in its royal household spoil the weather that men must experience, but there also has been involvement on an individual basis. Therefore, we can look for further developments along the lines of a connection between the fairy world and the mortal one.

The way in which Titania concludes her speech reminds us most strongly that the **theme** of love and marriage is the basis for this play. She says they are the parents of evil offspring - that is, since she has foresworn his bed and company, they do not produce children as would be the case were there marital harmony. Also, the amazed confusion of people who "know not which is which" when the seasons are all changed around is a significant description of the disorders and confusions caused by love problems. We should keep this phrasing in mind when future developments complicate our plot.

Oberon's answer to all of this is that the solution lies with Titania. There's no reason at all for her to quarrel with him. After all, he just wants a little changeling boy to be his "henchman" (page). His wheedling doesn't soften Titania, however. In her most queenly manner she denies him once again: "Set your heart at rest./ The fairyland buys not the child of me." Then she explains how she got the boy. His mother was a "vot'ress" (had taken a vow) in the order of which Titania was patroness.

They used to sit together on the yellow seashore and gossip. They would watch the trading ships sail out to sea and laugh when the wind made the canvas billow. Being pregnant with this boy, Titania's friend would imitate the ships and go fetch things from inland for Titania. She, being mortal, died giving birth to that boy, says Titania. And for her sake the Queen is bringing him up, and for her sake she will not part with him. After this moving and well-spoken explanation, Oberon asks only how long Titania plans to stay in that wood. Titania replies that she will probably stay till after Theseus is married. The Queen says if Oberon will be patient and participate harmoniously in her activities he should come with her. If not, then he ought to avoid her and she will do likewise. The stubborn King has only one objective. He will go with her if she will give him the boy. But Titania is of an equally firm disposition and she retorts, "Not for thy fairy kingdom." She bids her fairies away, saying she'll only quarrel more if she stays longer. With haughty splendor, she and her train leave. Oberon and Puck are now left to confer on the situation.

Oberon says to the departed Queen, well, if that's the way she wants it. Then he vows that before she leaves that wood, he'll torment her for the injury he considers she has done him. At this point he calls Puck to him. Oberon tells him to recall an occasion when the King sat on a promontory and heard a mermaid's song. His description is a high point in this play's poetry: the mermaid is on a dolphin's back, and she is "Uttering such dulcet and harmonious breath/ That the rude sea grew civil at her song,/ And certain stars shot madly from their spheres/ To hear the sea-maid's music." Puck replies that he remembers the incident. Oberon goes on to says that at that time he saw, though Puck could not, armed Cupid flying between the moon and the earth. Cupid took aim at "a fair vestal, throned by the west." He missed this target however. Oberon saw him shoot the love-arrow from his bow with the force to pierce a multitude of hearts. But the Fairy King could also see that the fiery shaft was "Quenched in the chaste beams of the wat'ry moon," missing the "imperial vot'ress," who went her way "In maiden meditation, fancy-free." Oberon saw where Cupid's arrow did fall. It hit "a little western flower," which had been white but after being hit turned purple. The name of this flower among maidens is "love-in-idleness." Oberon tells Puck to go out and get that flower for him, the one he once showed to him. The King explains that the juice of this flower, when put on the sleeping eyelids of man or woman, will cause the person to fall madly in love with the very first live creature that is seen upon waking, no matter who or what. Oberon repeats his instruction that Puck get this herb, saying the spirit should be back in less time than it takes a whale to swim a league. Puck replies that he will encircle the earth in forty minutes, and leaves to get the little flower. Beron, left alone, announces his intention in a soliloquy. Once he has this juice, he'll wait for an opportunity to put some on Titania's eyelids while she sleeps. Then, the very first thing she sees when she wakes - whether it's a lion, bear, wolf, bull, monkey, or ape - she shall be madly in love with to the depths of her soul. While she is in this condition of only having eyes for this creature, Oberon will be able to get the little changeling from her. Afterwards, when he has accomplished this goal, he can take the charm off her sight with another herb.

Comment

We should note first of all the great beauty of the poetry that Oberon and Titania speak. Oberon's speech about the beautiful music calming the sea and causing the stars to fall contributes to the whole statement this play is making about the power of art over life, and the important relation between love, art, beauty, "illusion" on the one hand and life, nature, "reality" on the other hand. Real reality cannot exclude the former terms.

The "fair vestal" and "imperial vot'ress" is Queen Elizabeth of England (throned by the West) who never married. In this **allusion**, the Virgin Queen is described as a votaress of Diana, the virgin moon-goddess. A vestal is a virgin priestess. "Fancy-free" means free of love thoughts. "Love-in-idleness" is another name for the pansy. The change from white to purple described in these lines may have been suggested by the change of the mulberries in the same way by the blood of Pyramus in Ovid's *Metamorphoses* (iv. 125-27).

Critics think that the **imagery** in this passage is reminiscent of an entertainment put on for Queen Elizabeth. Two entertainments have been suggested, either the one at Kenilworth in 1575 or that at Elvetham in 1591. The noted authority, Sir William Chambers, favors Elvetham, although he points out that all these pageants were very similar and that the special feature of a mermaid on a dolphin was not at either.

We should take note of how this play's special motifs, which we have pointed out and drawn attention to all along, appear all together in this crucial passage. First, the flower is hit by an arrow from Cupid's bow. Bows and arrows were mentioned previously.

The moon is an important presence in the scene. It is mentioned twice and has the special office of protecting the vestal maiden from Cupid's arrow by quenching the fiery shaft. Furthermore, we have remarked previous mentions of flowers and here the juice of a flower is given significant power. Also, transformation was discussed earlier and here the imperial vot'ress escapes the love metamorphosis, but the flower's resultant transformation is the cause of its power. Finally, this power that Oberon plans to use on Titania is of special significance. It rests on terms that have been previously and firmly established in the play: this juice affects the eyesight and controls one's vision of love. When these terms came up in combination earlier in our text, they were duly emphasized and should be recalled now that they re-enter here.

The combination of all these things prepares us for the importance that this love-juice does indeed have in our plot. Arrow, moon, flower, transformation, eyesight, are all signposts telling us to be alert for developments arising from what Oberon is starting here with this magic potion. And the very next thing that happens shows us we are not going to be disappointed.

As soon as Oberon finishes explaining his plan to use the love-juice on Titania, he notices two people approaching and wonders who they are. He declares that he will become invisible so that he can overhear their conversation. The two people are none other than Demetrius and Helena, who now enter with her following him. Demetrius is avowing that he does not love Helena and that she ought not to pursue him therefore. He wants to know where Lysander and Hermia are. Recall that Helena has told him of the planned elopement. He says he'll slay Lysander and that Hermia slays him. He reminds Helena that she told him they had stolen into this wood, "And," he says, "here am I, and wood within this wood," because he cannot find Hermia. (Wood means mad.) Demetrius concludes by brusquely ordering Helena off, telling her to follow him no more. Helena answers that he is like a magnet that draws her to him, except that her heart is not iron but steel, which is truer. She says if he'll stop having such magnetism, she'll stop following him. Demetrius asks if he entices her or speaks persuasively, then answers his own rhetorical questions by saying that he has told her straight out that he does not and cannot love her. Helena says she only loves him the more for that. She likens herself to the spaniel, which fawns on him the more he beats her. She asks that he use her only as a spaniel - spurn, strike, neglect, or lose her - only allow unworthy Helena to follow him. She says that's the lowest place she can ask for, to be used as his dog, but high enough for her. Demetrius warns her not to arouse too much hatred in him, and adds that it makes him sick to look at her. All Helena says to such abuse is that it makes her sick not to look at him. Then Demetrius points out the immodesty of her following him, leaving the city and putting herself at the mercy of someone who doesn't love her, when the darkness and the seclusion increase the threat to her virginity. Helena replies that his virtue is her protection, that his face lights the night for her, that he is all the world to her so she's not alone.

Demetrius says he'll run and hide, leaving her to the mercy of the wild beasts. She says he may do so, for he is worse than they could be. She adds that all tales of pursuit shall be turned around and the pursuer shall become the pursued - Daphne chase Apollo, the dove chase the griffin, the hind pursue the tiger - and how ridiculous is such a chase where cowardice pursues and valor flies. Demetrius says he won't listen any more, and if she continues to follow him, he warns that he will do some mischief to her in the wood. Helena agrees ironically, saying he does her mischief everywhere: temple, town, field. She concludes by calling his behavior scandalous, since he reverses the role of the sexes, making her do the wooing. Demetrius exits as Helena says, "We should be wooed, and were not made to woo." Then Helena herself leaves, saying she will follow him and that to die at his hand would be making a heaven of hell.

Oberon, who has been observing all that has passed between Demetrius and Helena, now says he will reverse that situation.

Before Demetrius leaves the wood, she will flee from him and he will pursue her. At this point, Puck enters, and Oberon asks if he has the flower with him and welcomes him back. Puck says he has it. Oberon asks him for it. Here follows another of the play's noteworthy passages of poetry. Oberon describes the place where Titania sleeps - "I know a bank where the wild thyme blows" - and he names all the flowers that surround her. He adds that there also the snake sheds her skin, a garment big enough for a fairy's outfit. While Titania sleeps there, Oberon will put this juice on her eyes, which will make her "full of hateful fantasies." Oberon then tells Puck to take some juice too, and go looking through the woods for a couple of Athenians. The lady is in love and the youth disdains her, and so, says Oberon, anoint the youth's eyes when the next thing he sees is the lady. Oberon tells Puck he may recognize the youth by his Athenian clothes. He instructs his spirit to be especially careful so that the youth may be more in love with the lady than she with him. Oberon's concluding words instruct Puck to meet him before the cock crows. Puck's reassurance that he will do so closes this scene.

Comment

When Oberon declares, "I am invisible," he is entitled by Elizabethan stage **convention** to remain on the stage without being seen by any other characters who may enter. Sometimes a character would put on a black cloak and by this the audience was to understand that he could not be seen by other people on stage.

When Demetrius says he is wood in the wood, he begins a series of puns on the locale of the play which is added to by Helena at line 242 when she says women should be wooed. Wood meaning forest, wood meaning mad, and woo'd or wooed meaning courted are meaningfully connected in this play.

Helena's remarks on the lowly place of the spaniel and their abject servility should be noted because of Shakespeare's repeated reference to these animals in this way. When Helena speaks of traditional her suit stories being turned around, we have another instance of the transformation **theme**. Daphne fled from Apollo and was changed into a laurel tree. The griffin is a mythical beast with the head of an eagle and the body of a lion. A hind is a doe. Reversing the role of the sexes and changing hell into heaven are remarks by Helena which also serve to recall the play's concern with the **theme** of transformation.

Oberon's concluding speech names six different flowers just for the pleasure of recounting them: thyme, oxslip, violet, woodbine, musk-rose, and eglantine. All this is not needed for a mere identification of Titania's bower. The snake-skin big enough for a fairy is a colorful detail serving to remind us of the diminutive size of these creatures. By the end of the speech we see how the affairs of the fairies are going to have a bearing on the lovers.

SUMMARY

In this scene we learn of the quarrel between Oberon and Titania. The plot of the former for the latter begins to weave in with the predicament of the lovers, because Oberon witnesses Helena's one-sided affection and determines to remedy this. The following should be noted about this scene:

(1) Oberon and Titania speak poetry of great beauty. Puck's poetry is remarkable for rough vigor and a rustic flavor all its own. It contrasts with the delicacy of the fairy songs. When Demetrius and Helena enter they are still speaking in the uninteresting, wooden way we have already

seen. This contrasts markedly with the flexibility and grace of the poetry given to the fairies.

(2) The scene opens and closes with a speech about flowers. At least nine different flowers are mentioned in this scene alone: pansy ("little western flower"), cowslip, rose, wild thyme, oxslip, violet, woodbine, musk-rose, eglantine.

(3) There have been a multitude of references to the **theme** of change and transformation. The following major instances ought to be remembered:

(a) The quarrel between Oberon and Titania is over a "changeling."

(b) Not only the cause but the result of the quarrel concerns change - the seasons have become all turned around.

(c) The solution to the quarrel is possible because of a change in a little flower that occurred at the same time that the Virgin Queen did not change.

(d) The power of this changed flower is to transform love-sight.

In general, the moon, which presides over the whole play, is constantly changing from one phase to another. Both love and art look to the moon as their sovereign star. Art transforms reality. And we have been told over and over that love has to do not with constancy but with change.

BRIGHT NOTES STUDY GUIDE

ACT 2: SCENE 2

This scene takes place in another part of the woods. Titania enters with her attendants. She bids them dance and sing and then go perform their various duties. Some will kill worms ("cankers") in flowers, some will fight with bats ("reremice") for their wings out of which elves' coats shall be made, some will keep back the noisy owl that nightly hoots at them. First they must sing her asleep, then do the above jobs. The fairies then sing their song. It is a lullaby, consisting of two four-line **tetrameter stanzas** and a six-line chorus. In it, snakes, hedgehogs, newts, and blindworms (small snakes) are told not to come near the Fairy Queen. Then the chorus calls on Philomela, the nightingale, to come and sing in this lullaby for the Queen. The closing lines of the chorus ask that no harm, spell or charm, come near the lovely Titania. The second **stanza** warns off spiders, beetles, worms, and snails, and is followed by the same chorus as above.

During the second chorus, Titania falls asleep. The fairies depart to perform the tasks she assigned, leaving one of their band as sentinel. When they have left, Oberon enters and squeezes the flower which Puck brought to him on Titania's eyelids. The King incants a charm over her while doing this. Like the fairies' lullaby, it is in rhymed **tetrameter** lines. It says that whatever she sees upon waking she will fall in love with, whether ounce (lynx), cat, bear, pard (leopard), or bristly boar. No matter what it is, in her eyes it will appear beloved, and Oberon concludes by wishing she wake when some vile thing is near. Then he exits.

Comment

All of the poetry is in the uniquely light and graceful style created by Shakespeare to express the nature of these special creatures. The duties that Titania details to her crew add to our information about this fairy world. Using bats' wings for elves' coats emphasizes once again their small size. The fairies' lullaby specifically tries to ward off spells and charms, but the very next thing that happens is Oberon's putting a charm on Titania. The lullaby names eight small animals and insects, plus the nightingale. Oberon's incantation over the sleeping Titania when he puts the love-juice on her eyes adds six large animals to this list. The former song asks that nothing come near the Queen; the latter song asks that something does come near, the viler the better. The approach of humans is not covered by either song.

After Oberon has left Titania sleeping with the love-juice on her eyelids, Lysander and Hermia enter. They are trying to execute their plan to elope to Lysander's aunt's house. Lysander speaks, remarking that Hermia is weak from wandering in the woods and admits that he has forgotten how to get to their destination. He suggests that if Hermia is agreeable, they'll rest where they are and await daylight. Hermia agrees, says she will rest right there and he ought to go look for a place for himself. Lysander suggests that they sleep on the same turf since their hearts are betrothed to each other. Hermia says no to this, telling him twice to lie further off. Lysander says his intentions are pure and innocent and then he speaks of how their two hearts are really one so she ought not to deny him a sleeping place at her side. Lying thus, he does not lie, says Lysander. Hermia compliments him on his riddling and says she never meant to accuse him of being a liar, but she still insists that he lie further off for modesty's sake. She wants enough space left between them, as society deems proper between a bachelor and a maid. She bids him good night and wishes his love never alter till the end of his life. Lysander adds Amen to that, saying may his life end when his loyalty to her does. He lies down and prays that sleep come to her. Hermia wishes him the same and they both sleep.

Comment

We have been expecting Hermia and Lysander to put in an appearance because (a) we knew they planned to meet in the wood to embark on their elopement and (b) we saw Demetrius and Helena at the end of the last scene and Demetrius spoke of the elopement, demanding of Helena the whereabouts of Lysander and Hermia. One would have expected Lysander to lose the way to auntie's house. Not only is it a stock fairy-tale plot complication, but also Lysander does not inspire one with confidence in his ability. His riddling and smooth-talking here show him to be a rather silly and shallow youth, harmless enough but withal a fatuous nonentity in terms of dramatic characterization. Note the confident assertions of unaltered loyalty to his love, Hermia. Hermia hopes he'll love her till he dies. Lysander takes this statement and goes right out on a limb with it, saying he hopes to die when he ceases to love her.

While Hermia and Lysander lie asleep, Puck enters. Recall that Oberon had given him some love-juice to remedy the situation Helena was in with the unloving Demetrius, which the King witnessed. He told Puck to look for a youth with Athenian garments on and put the charm on him. Now Puck says he has gone through the forest without being able to find this Athenian to put the magic juice on. Then he spies Lysander and sees his Athenian clothes. He shouts with joy at gaining the object of his search, saying this must be whom Oberon meant, the Athenian youth who despises the maid. Then he sees Hermia, assuming she is the suffering maiden, and remarking how she dare not lie close to this nasty man -

A MIDSUMMER NIGHT'S DREAM

this "lack-love," "kill-courtesy," "churl" (boor). Consequently, Puck casts all the power of the love-charm on Lysander, bidding love take over his eyes and that he wake when Puck is gone. The spirit departs to rejoin Oberon. As soon as he has left, Demetrius and Helena enter at a run. She is begging him to stay, even though he kill her. He bids her be off and stop haunting him. She begs him not to leave her in the dark thus. But Demetrius leaves alone, threatening her with peril if she doesn't stay where she is.

Helena is now by herself and she says she is out of breath with this foolish pursuit, and the more she prays the less she gets. She compares herself to Hermia, happy wherever she may be, and speaks of the beauty of her eyes in particular. Helena says that tears did not make Hermia's eyes so bright because her own are more often washed that way. She says she is as ugly as a bear and it's no wonder that Demetrius flees from her, since all the beasts do. It was absurd of her to compare her eyes to Hermia's. At this point Helena sees Lysander on the ground. She cannot tell if he be dead or asleep and to find out, she awakens him. Of course, Lysander has the love juice on his eyes so when he awakens and sees Helena he immediately declares his great love for her. He says he will run through fire for her. He calls her "transparent Helena," saying he can see her heart through her bosom. He asks her where Demetrius is, calls him vile, and ends with the fiery statement that such a man is fit to die on his sword. Helena tells Lysander not to talk that way about Demetrius, even though the latter does love Hermia. For, says Helena, Hermia still loves Lysander and that should content him. Lysander forcefully denies that he could be content with Hermia. He says he repents the time he has spent with the latter; he loves Helena, not Hermia, having had the good sense to change a raven for a dove. He then dwells at length on how this change from one love to another is an instance of his reason governing his will. Reason has told him Helena is worthier, his reason was not ripe till now, but now that it is ripe it is governing his will. And that's why he loves Helena. His reason leads him to her eyes where he reads love's stories in love's richest book. Helena is quite taken aback by all this and she assumes that Lysander is making fun of her and scorning her. She asks, isn't it enough she has so much trouble with Demetrius, but he should thus torment her for her insufficiency. She says he does her great wrong to woo her thus in jest - she thought he was better bred than that. She says farewell, and leaves lamenting that she should be refused by one man and abused by another because of that refusal.

Comment

Now things are really beginning to happen. Oberon's instructions to Puck did not take into account that there were two Athenian youths in the wood, and so his mode of identifying Demetrius was not sufficient. The big issue Hermia made over not sleeping too near Lysander is now seen to have important results:

(a) Puck knows the youth he's looking for despises the maid who loves him. When he sees Lysander and Hermia lying at some distance from each other, it is supporting evidence for his mistaken identification of the youth as Demetrius.

(b) When Helena comes on the scene, she can awaken Lysander without awakening Hermia also. Thus Puck's mistake can have the outcome it does.

(c) Since Helena does not see Hermia, she can't turn to her for an explanation. Furthermore, Hermia doesn't observe the situation either.

We should note the convenient coincidences that are operating here in that as soon as Lysander has been prepared and Puck has left, Demetrius and Helena appear. Then Helena is left alone to encounter Lysander alone. Neither Demetrius nor Hermia sees what happens. When Helena and Demetrius enter, even though they are running, and their words are very urgent indeed, the form they speak in is that very formal "stichomythia" explained earlier (characters speak single alternating lines that **rhyme** with each other two by two). When Demetrius leaves after four lines of this kind of alternating dialogue, Helena continues to speak of her woeful plight in rhymed couplets. This pretty formality casts the action into the proper key - this is not a stark tragedy but a romantic comedy. We should note that Helena dwells on the subject of eyes, comparing her own and Hermia's. A long list of animals entered our **imagery** earlier in this scene and here too a bear is mentioned when poor Helena says she must look like one. She mentions beasts and monsters also.

Her speaking in rhymed **couplets** is the source of great comedy when she awakens Lysander, because the last line of her speech begins a **couplet** that is finished by the extravagant avowal of love he pops out with as soon as he opens his eyes. Helena: "Lysander, if you live, good sir, awake." Lysander, starting up: "And run through fire I will for thy sweet sake." The absurdity of this protestation is heightened by this trick with the **rhyme**. After all, the last thing Lysander said before dropping off to sleep was that he would die if ever he stopped loving Hermia. And here he is, making the most extravagant love vows to another girl, and rhyming them instantly at that. No matter if he's just been awakened from a deep sleep - this is like a musical comedy routine where, at the drop of a hat, everybody in sight suddenly performs synchronized dance-steps in harmonizing pastel costumes. And there is more comedy to come, for the enchanted Lysander now chooses to explain his actions as based on reason. While we know he is just a puppet on a string, he goes on and on about how his will is at last being properly governed by his mature reason. We laugh in the security of our superior knowledge, but we must reserve judgment until the play has completed its statement about love and judgment, will and reason, vision and eyesight, illusion and reality. We may still laugh at Lysander but we may also laugh at ourselves, knowing a little more because we have realized that we know a lot less.

Lysander compares Hermia to a raven and Helena to a dove. Hermia was played by a dark actor and Helena by a light. Future remarks will substantiate this and we will also be told that Helena is tall and Hermia short.

After Helena's departure, Lysander remarks that she has not seen Hermia. He bids Hermia stay sleeping where she is and he wishes she may never come near him. He likens her to a sweet food of which he has had a surfeit and to a false belief which is hated when no longer held. He says, may she be hated by all, but most of all by him. He concludes by vowing all his love and strength to the honor and protection of Helena, and then leaves. Hermia awakens when he has left and cries to him for help, asking him to pluck a serpent from her breast. She has had a dream that a serpent was eating her heart and that Lysander looked upon the cruelty with a smile. She is still quaking with fear. She calls his name twice, asks where he might be, bids him speak, and finally ascertaining that he is not anywhere near, she leaves to find him or to die if not.

Comment

Lysander's words to Hermia are needlessly cruel and her terror when she wakes is justified by his behavior towards her, though its immediate cause is her bad dream. Her mention of a serpent continues the **allusions** to animals in this scene, as did Lysander's mention of a raven and a dove. With Hermia's exit here the merry chase is on: she is looking for Lysander who is pursuing Helena who is following Demetrius who is searching for Hermia.

SUMMARY

This scene has accomplished the following:

(1) Titania's eyes have been enchanted and she awaits being awakened by her destined "beloved."

(2) Puck has mistaken Lysander for Demetrius and ham put the charm on him so that now Lysander loves Helena.

(3) The situation is now worsened from the beginning, because neither man loves the woman who loves him. Hermia loves Lysander who loves Helena who loves Demetrius who loves Hermia. The fairies dance their rounds and ringlets and roundels, and the lovers too prance unwittingly in a circle.

A MIDSUMMER NIGHT'S DREAM

TEXTUAL ANALYSIS

ACT 3

ACT 3: SCENE 1

This scene takes place in the wood near Titania's bower. The Athenian workmen enter: Quince, Snug, Bottom, Flute, Snout, and Starveling. They have come to rehearse their play as they planned to do in Act 1, Scene 2. Bottom is the first to speak and he asks if they are all present. Quince says yes and that the spot they're in is a good place for their rehearsal. It has a clear plot to serve as a stage, and a hawthorn hedge to serve as a dressing room. They will do it just as they intend to before the Duke. Bottom here addresses Quince, who turns his attention to his friend, "bully Bottom." Bottom wishes to call Quince's attention to certain things in their play which will never please its audience. First, Pyramus must kill himself with his sword - the ladies will not be able to stand that. Bottom wants to know what's to be done about it. Snout agrees that it is a "parlous" (perilous, terrible) fear, and Starveling thinks they'll have to leave the killing out of the final production. But no, the resourceful Bottom has a ready solution. He says he must recite a prologue that explains everything: their swords do no harm, Pyramus is not dead really, and in fact Pyramus is really Bottom the Weaver. In short, the prologue must declare that all the make-believe is merely make-believe. Then, says Bottom, the audience will not be afraid. Quince agrees to such a prologue and suggests it be written in "eight and six" (lines of eight and six syllables alternating, which is the common **ballad** meter). Bottom cannot resist adding the last touch, so he says it should be written in eight-syllable lines entirely. Snout asks, won't the ladies be afraid of the lion. Starveling, for one, fears just that result. Bottom says very grandly that they ought to consider very carefully bringing in "a lion among ladies." He says, "there is not a more fearful wild-fowl than your lion living," and it requires some attention. Snout unoriginally suggests another prologue. But Bottom again comes up with the solution that works. The lion costume should not entirely conceal the actor wearing it and he must announce that the lion really isn't one, then say his name is Snug the joiner.

This plan Quince agrees to and he brings up two more production problems. Thisbe and Pyramus are supposed to meet by moonlight, and also they must talk through a wall. First moonlight is discussed. Snout asks if the moon shines the night of the play, and Bottom calls for an almanac to find out. Quince says, yes, it does. Bottom says then they may leave a window open during their performance and the moonlight will come into the chamber that way. Quince says yes to this idea, adding as an alternative that a man may present moonshine with a lantern and a thorn bush.

Then Quince states the second production problem: Pyramus and Thisbe are supposed to talk through a chink in a wall. Snout doesn't see how they can possibly satisfy this requirement and he asks Bottom's opinion. The indomitable Bottom has the answer. It is based on Quince' idea for moonshine - let a man with plaster, loam, or roughcast on him stand for a wall and he can hold his fingers up for Pyramus and Thisbe to talk through as a chink. Quince agrees that in such a fashion they may solve their production problems. He then begins the rehearsal, calling for Pyramus first. After speaking, everyone shall enter the hawthorn hedge on cue.

Comment

The great pains that our simple workmen take to explain away every illusion offers another comment on the reality/illusion **theme** at the heart of this play. To these men, reality and illusion are two entirely separate entities, and they insist upon stating which is which at every point where the slightest confusion might arise. They take absolutely no chances on this question. The manner in which their production goes forward is a classic expression of the position they represent on this question.

Their production difficulties concerning the moonshine that is required also serve to draw attention once again to this important ingredient in our play's magic. But we should notice that when Bottom and his fellows deal with the moon, even that evanescent, inconstant body is brought down to earth and made to conform to their no-nonsense **realism**. Better have one of their own company represent moon than leave the matter up to that fleeting, shifting natural phenomenon.

The reference to "a lion among ladies" is thought to refer to a royal baptismal celebration at which a lion was to have drawn a carriage in the procession. But a blackamoor had to be substituted because the ladies present were frightened. This similarity to a historical event is used as evidence in assigning a date to this play.

After Quince has explained the rehearsal procedure and called on Pyramus to begin, Puck enters. He wonders aloud, "What hempen homespuns have we swagg'ring here, / So near the cradle of the Fairy Queen?" He sees it is a play rehearsal and says he'll watch and perhaps act too if he sees the opportunity. He is not seen by anyone. Quince now directs Pyramus to speak and Thisbe to stand forth. In his first line, Pyramus (Bottom) says "odious" instead of "odors" and Quince corrects him. Bottom makes the correction incorrectly, and continues till he must exit to investigate a noise he hears. Puck comments on what a strange Pyramus Bottom makes and he exits too. Thisbe (Flute) asks if it is his turn to speak. Quince explains that it is, Pyramus having just gone to "see a noise that he heard" and that he will be back. Then Thisbe speaks, praising her Pyramus in flower terms and saying she will meet him at "Ninny's tomb." Quince corrects this to "Ninus' tomb," adding that Flute is not supposed to speak that yet - that's supposed to be in answer to Pyramus. Flute has spoken his part all at once, cues and all. Quince calls for Bottom to enter, saying his cue is past. Thisbe repeats Bottom's cue and at this point Pyramus re-enters and lo he has the head of an ass in place of his human one. Puck accompanies him. Quince shouts out his dismay: "O monstrous! O strange! We are haunted." They all flee in terror from the transformed Bottom, leaving him alone. Puck leaves in order to further torment the terrorized tradesmen. The spirit says he'll assume various animal shapes - horse, hound, hog, headless bear, fire too - and lead the deranged Athenians a merry chase through bog, bush, brake, briar, while he makes all the appropriate animal sounds.

Left alone, Bottom, who does not realize what Puck has done to him, expresses his own amazement at the behavior of his fellows. Since he doesn't know his own condition, he wonders why they have run away from him. He decides that they are playing a practical joke on him and trying to make him afraid. Here Snout re-enters and exclaims, "O Bottom, thou art changed! what do I see on thee?" Bottom's answer is that Snout sees an ass-head of his own. Snout leaves and then Quince re-enters and exclaims in turn, "Bless thee, Bottom! bless thee! thou art translated." When Quince has left again and the bewildered Bottom is alone, he resolutely confronts his situation and analyzes thus: "I see their knavery: this is to make an ass of me; to fright me, if they could." He decides that he'll show them he's not afraid - he'll stay right where he is and not run after them. And furthermore, to show most plainly his courage in the face of adversity, he'll walk around and sing so they'll hear that he's not afraid.

Comment

With Puck's chance entrance upon the workmen's rehearsal, the fairy plot begins to interweave with the workmen's affairs. In the preceding scene, the fairy world began affecting the lovers' affairs. We must watch the progressive interweaving of these threads. Notice how extensively flowers figure in the dialogue of "Pyramus and Thisbe." We have pointed out before how this is a continuing motif. Existing right alongside this element in the play's atmosphere is a very contrasting type of **imagery**: Puck's cataloguing of the animals he'll imitate to frighten the workmen and his graphic recital of the rough sound-effects with which he'll pursue them. We have pointed out this contrast between the delicacy and light airiness of the fairy language on the one hand and Puck's homey, rough style on the other.

Ninus' tomb is the rendezvous of Pyramus and Thisbe in Ovid. Ninus was the mythical founder of Nineveh; his wife Semiramis was supposed to have built the walls of Babylon, at which place the scene of the story of Pyramus and Thisbe is laid. Quince's difficulty with his actors - that they speak everything together, cues and dialogue - is the classic problem of the director of amateur theatricals.

Bottom's transformation brings to a **climax** this important **theme** in the play, whose emergence we have noted in many places. His transformation will work together with the other **climax** of this **theme** - the transformation produced by the little western flower - to produce the play's complete statement about reality and illusion, life and love. When Snout and Quince use the words "changed" and "translated," we are meant to remember all the times, and they are many, that these words have appeared in our text. At the end of Act 2, Scene 1, we summarized some of the major instances.

Bottom does not know that he has been given the head of an ass by Puck when he twice mentions being an ass. He is merely speaking metaphorically of his condition. Of course, our knowing position makes these comments of his very ironical.

Really frightened and bewildered, but resolutely disclaiming this Bottom bravely "whistles in the dark" to keep his spirits up in the face of such perplexing behavior on the part of his companions. He therefore walks back and forth and sings a song about a "woosel cock," a "throstle," and a "wren with little quill." His singing wakes me Titania, who has been sleeping nearby, and she says, "What angel wakes me from my flow'ry bed?"

Bottom continues undaunted, singing another verse about several more birds: finch, sparrow, lark, and cuckoo. (The "plainsong" of the last is noticed by many and they cannot say "nay" to it). Bottom comments on this last fact in his song, saying it is indeed useless to refute a foolish bird, even though he may be wrong. Now Titania is awake, and with eyes enchanted by the love-juice, she has seen Bottom. Consequently she says will he please sing some more, for she loves to hear him. In fact, she continues, she loves to look at him also. Her words are ironical here, because she doesn't know how very true they are, but we do: "So is mine eye enthralled to thy shape," says the poor deluded Queen. To this "hempen homespun" crowned with the head of an ass, the Queen of Fairies says that his "fair virtue's force" (the compelling attraction of his manly charms) causes her on first sight to swear she loves him.

Bottom answers her with the same unswerving **realism** he applied to the last line of his song. He tells her with plain and beautiful truth that she has little reason for that avowal. He adds the comment that reason and love "keep little company together nowadays," and it's too bad they don't get together. He comments on this observation, saying that he can "gleek" sometimes (make biting jests). Titania's response exhibits the superfluity of her passion - "Thou art as wise as thou art beautiful," she proclaims. Her excessiveness contrast with Bottom's true and solid declarations, and he himself catches her up on this foolishness, saying abruptly, "Not so." But, he adds, if he were wise enough to get out of the wood, that would be wise enough for him. Now the Queen in Titania reasserts itself, as she says with all the authority of her high position, "Out of this wood do not desire to go." She tells Bottom that he will stay whether he wants to or not, and she explains that she is a powerful spirit on whose commands the summer itself depends. And she loves him. Thus he will go with her and she will have fairies wait upon him. Bottom will sleep on flowers while they sing, and, she concludes, she will "purge thy mortal grossness so" that Bottom will become like an airy spirit. At this point she calls her four fairies to attend on Bottom: Peaseblossom, Cobweb, Moth, and Mustardseed.

Comment

A "woosel" or ouzel is the English blackbird or merle, of the thrush family. A "throstle" is a song thrush or marvis. A "quill" is a pipe made of a reed or stalk and here refers to the wren's song. "Plainsong" means a simple and unvarying song. In the case of the cuckoo, this sounds like cuckold, so many a man hearing this applied to him cannot deny it.

We should note that Bottom's remarks on reason and love are very correct statements of what happens in this play. Saying that he would be sufficiently wise if he had wit enough to get out of this wood is a clever statement because wood also means mad, as was pointed out earlier.

When Puck came in and announced that Bottom and his fellows were near the bower of Titania, the plot development became obvious. But no matter if the coincidence s extravagant, the sight of Titania in love with the ass-headed Bottom loses none of its effect. The names of the fairies that Titania calls are in keeping with the tiny, airy, delicate creatures Shakespeare has created in this play.

The four fairies enter at Titania's call and each in turn announces that he is ready, then in chorus ask where she wants them to go. Titania then lists all the services she wants them to perform for her beloved Bottom. They must accompany him courteously and kindly, feeding him with fruits-apricots, dewberries, purple grapes, green figs, and mulberries. They should steal honey from the bumblebees for him, and to light his way at night they will ignite torches from the glow-worm's eyes. She instructs them to pluck butterfly's wings to fan the moonbeams from his eyes as he sleeps. At her behest, each fairy says, "Hail, mortal!" Bottom gently returns the greeting and courteously inquires each elf's name. He has a friendly comment upon each name. To Cobweb he says he will use him if he cuts his finger (cobweb was used to staunch blood). To Peaseblossom he says he wishes to be commended to Mistress Squash, his mother, and to Master Peascod, his father (a squash is an unripe pea pod and a peascod is a ripe pea pod). To Mustardseed he mentions the well-known patience associated with him and says also that mustardseed has caused his eyes to water (referring to the spice). To all the elves he has said that he looks forward to knowing them better.

Comment

Titania's speech adds to our information about the fairy world that Shakespeare has created in this play. The activities described here paint an extraordinary scene of the whimsical, delightful, non-mortal world that Shakespeare has brought into being in this play. The list of foods-fruits and honey-is as beautiful as the many lists of flowers we have had before. We should note that moonbeams cannot be excluded from the scene.

Bottom's easy graciousness with his extraordinary new companions is a mark of his marvelous ability to adapt immediately to whatever life offers him. His energetic love of life, his naiveté and eager innocence obtain his entrance into this other-world so different from his own. And he enjoys it to the fullest.

Titania now closes the scene by telling her elves to lead Bottom to her bower. She says the moon looks watery and

A MIDSUMMER NIGHT'S DREAM

when this happens the flowers weep, lamenting "some enforced chastity" (violated chastity). Bring him quietly, she orders, and they all leave.

Comment

Titania's last words strike once again the keynote in this play's special atmosphere. She mentions:

(1) the moon

(2) flowers

(3) love problems

SUMMARY

This scene accomplishes the following major things:

(1) The manner in which the Athenian workmen treat their play amplifies the relationship between illusion and reality-a **theme** at the heart of the play as a whole. These men are very certain which is which and they impose this attitude on their performance of "Pyramus and Thisbe." The result is comic in itself and is also in marked contrast to the confusions on this subject everywhere else in the play.

(2) Puck enters this world of simple **realism** and creates havoc by placing the head of an ass on Bottom. They have just been at great pains to show the man behind the lion's costume in their play and then Puck steps in and their very own bully Bottom is entirely changed into an ass from the neck up with no man showing to reassure them at all. If

such can happen in their solidly real world, then there are no limits possible to be fixed for sure between illusion and reality.

(3) The fantastically transformed Bottom, the least likely candidate for the role in the world before his transformation, now becomes a participator in the fairy world in the incredible position of being Titania's beloved. But we see that it was possible after all, indeed it seems an absolutely necessary liaison once we see how naturally Bottom takes to it. He conducts himself with such sobriety and yet such grace, with his own good sense and yet with such enjoyment that we see that Bottom the weaver is supremely capable of uniting these disparate worlds. His love of life enables him to engage in it to the fullest. The fullness of his engagement unites experience. The union of reality and illusion empower him and are embodied in him.

ACT 3: SCENE 2

This scene takes place in another part of the same wood. Oberon enters and wonders out loud what it was that Titania fell in love with under the charm he put on her. Puck enters and Oberon asks him what "night rule" prevails in this "haunted grove." Puck launches right into a description of what he has done to Bottom and the other workmen and how Titania now loves a "monster." He says that near her bower where she lay asleep "a crew of patches, rude mechanicals" came to rehearse a play for Theseus' wedding celebration. Puck describes Bottom as "the shallowest thick skin of that barren sort" and tells Oberon how, when the workman went behind a hedge, he put an ass's head on him. He describes the havoc this caused among the other workmen when they saw their companion, in terms drawn from hunting - they scattered like wild geese or choughs at a gun shot. Puck continues in his characteristically graphic, rough and homey style to paint the disorder he created with his prank. And finally, says he, the "translated" Pyramus (Bottom), thus deserted by his terrified companions, is seen by the enchanted Titania: "Titania waked and straightway loved an ass."

Oberon says he is more than pleased with this result. He goes on to ask if Puck put the love-juice on the Athenian (meaning Demetrius). Puck says yes to this, and that the woman was nearby so he woke in love with her as Oberon intended (but Puck really enchanted Lysander by mistake). At this point, Hermia and Demetrius enter. Oberon says that here is the Athenian he spoke of. Puck, of course, says that this is the woman, but not the man. Then his mistake becomes evident, for of course these two discuss their situation. Demetrius left Helena before she awakened Lysander and was beloved of him by the power of the juice, so he knows nothing of that event. Lysander left Hermia sleeping when he set off to follow Helena, so Hermia is also completely in the dark on that score. All Demetrius knows is that Helena told him of the planned elopement and he wants Hermia for himself and has been searching for her. Now he has found her and he protests his great love for her as usual. She, of course, wants to know what has happened to her true love, Lysander, who had been sleeping by her side. He would never leave her and she accuses Demetrius of killing him. Lysander was as true to her as the sun to the day, she says, and she would as soon believe that the moon could go through the center of the earth and shine in the daytime on the other side, as believe that Lysander would thus leave her. Demetrius must have murdered him. Demetrius still plays his love game, saying he's the one who's murdered by Hermia's cruelty to him.

Yet she's as beautiful as "yonder Venus in her glimmering sphere," even though she's a murderer. Poor Hermia has no patience with Demetrius's love prattle now. She wants her Lysander, and begs Demetrius for him. Demetrius replies that he would sooner give Lysander's carcass to his hounds than give him to Hermia. She can't stand this and reviles him thoroughly, begging him to speak the truth for once, and not be a double-tongued serpent, killer of a sleeping man. At this passionate outburst, Demetrius ceases his sweet talk and avows he neither killed him nor has any reason to think he is dead. Hermia begs him to reassure her. At her soft plea, Demetrius' designs on her reassert themselves and he callously asks what his reward will be for doing what she asks. Hermia's anger returns at his suggestive, leering remark and she says his reward is to never see her again. No matter how worried she is about Lysander, she'll stand no more of Demetrius's unpleasantness. She leaves and Demetrius remarks that it will do no good to plead his suit while she's in this temper, so he'll sleep there for awhile. Before doing so, he says a few pretty words on the subject. He then lies down and sleeps.

Comment

We should note the gusto and vigor of Puck's inimitable style. He really enjoys recounting his mischief to his master, Oberon, and his vivid description of the poor "mechanicals" is one of the poetic high points of the play. We should also note that both Hermia and Demetrius cannot keep from mentioning the moon - the influence of this body is too pervasive ever to be absent. The way each uses it is very different, however. An indication that in this play the moon lends itself appropriately to any and every occasion. When Demetrius really angers her, Hermia's language becomes truly passionate and expressive of great feeling.

Demetrius now lies asleep, and Oberon has been made fully aware of Puck's mistake. He says as much to him-Puck has turned a true love into a false one and has not turned any false love true. Puck says it's the rule of fate that for every man who keeps his oath, a million break them. Oberon instructs him to go swiftly through the wood and find Helena of Athens, whom he describes as pale and lovelorn. Bring her by some illusion, says Oberon, and meanwhile Demetrius will be charmed with the love-juice in preparation for her appearance so that he will wake and love her. Puck sings that his departure is swifter that an arrow from a Tartar's bow, and he is off on his errand. Oberon then chants the charm over the sleeping Demetrius: the flower that was hit by Cupid's archery shall cause Demetrius to see Helena shining as gloriously as Venus in the sky. Puck re-enters and tells Oberon that Helena is close by. She is accompanied by Lysander, whom he mistook for Demetrius, and the spectacle they present is well worth watching, the mischievous spirit tells his master. "Lord, what fools these mortals be!" is Puck's famous reaction to the sight of Lysander pleading for Helena's love. Oberon says they must get out of the way, for the sound of Lysander's and Helena's voices will awaken Demetrius. Puck is delighted at the prospect of both men loving Helena at once. He loves preposterous things best, and this will really be something.

Lysander and Helena now enter. He is protesting the truth of his love vows, saying his tears prove that he is not wooing in scorn. Helena insists he's just being cunning. His vow belong to Hermia, and when he makes them to Helena they cancel each other out-his vows amount to nothing. Lysander says he had no judgment when he vowed his love to Hermia. Helena wisely observes that he has none now when he gives Hermia up. Lysander's next argument is that Demetrius loves Hermia and does not love Helena. At this crucial moment Demetrius wakes and immediately declares his great love for Helena in the most extravagant language. He calls her goddess, nymph, perfect, divine; he says her eyes are clearer than crystal, her lips more red than cherries, her hand more white than high mountain snow. Helena is understandably confounded by this declaration. In fact, she's outraged. "O spite! O hell!" she exclaims. She's of the confirmed opinion that they have joined together to make fun of her. She had earlier thought Lysander alone was making fun of her when he declared his undying devotion- now she suspects a league against her. She says, can't they merely hate her without so abusing her? It is not manly of them to carry on so as if they loved her when she knows they hate her. They are really rivals for Hermia's love and now they're just trying to outdo each other in mocking Helena. How low of them to make her cry with their derision, she says. No noble person would so torment and offend a young maid just to have the fun of it.

Lysander now takes it upon himself to reprimand Demetrius, saying that since he loves Hermia, Lysander will give over his claim to that girl. In exchange he'll take Helena, whom he now loves till his death. Helena here interjects her opinion of this as idle mockery and a waste of breath. Now Demetrius has his say, which is, of course, that Lysander can keep his Hermia. He only liked her temporarily, and now his affection has returned home to Helena for good. Lysander tells Helena not to believe Demetrius. Demetrius warns him to keep his opinion to himself, and points out to Lysander that his beloved Hermia is approaching. At this point Hermia, who knows nothing of all the latest goings on, enters. All she knows is that her Lysander disappeared from her side while she was asleep.

Comment

Before the confusion in this foursome reaches its peak by the addition of the fourth member, let us note some points about the preceding developments. Puck's observation that the proportion of constant men to inconstant men is one to a million recalls the many earlier statements on man's inconstancy. Remember that Hermia swore to meet Lysander "by all the vows that ever men have broke," which is many more than women have ever made. And both Oberon and Theseus have a long history of amours. Even though the confusion is immediately caused by Puck's mistake, his opinion is that men in love are ridiculous anyway: "Lord, what fools these mortals be!"

Archery (Tartar's bow; Cupid's archery) and the moon (Venus in the sky) should be noted as recurrent here. Lysander's claim to judgment in loving Helena now, as opposed to having had none when he loved Hermia before, reminds us again of this issue (the relationship between judgment and love). Demetrius wakes up exactly on cue, as Lysander is telling Helena that her beloved Demetrius doesn't love her, so why shouldn't she take Lysander as a substitute. And of course, enchanted as he is, Demetrius immediately spouts the most absurdly extravagant love-vows the minute he opens his eyes. He is utterly ridiculous. The first part of her that he chooses to praise is, ironically, her eyes. It is to be noted that Helena's reactions are very feelingly expressed and she becomes much more real to us as a character. In contrast to this, the two men still speak their customary wooden language, full of formal twists and turns on words - the same shallow tripe. Lysander wants to just swap girls with Demetrius - it's as simple as that, he says. Lysander's last words to Hermia were that he would love her till his death. Now he turn right around and says the same about Helena. The enchanted Demetrius is equally ridiculous: now, says he, I really know what I'm doing, so I've come back to Helena. In short, what we have here is the exact reverse of the initial situation when both men loved Hermia. At this point, both Lysander and Demetrius are madly in love with Helena, and nobody loves Hermia. The women haven't budged an inch - each loves her own man as always.

Now Hermia, who has been searching for her beloved Lysander, enters. All she knows is that she woke from a bad dream and found him gone. She has seen Demetrius since, but he was no help. He just annoyed her with his usual persistent wooing. When she finds out what's going on, the confusion will reach its hilarious peak. Hermia begins very sedately by observing that in the darkness her eyes didn't help her find Lysander, but her ears were more acute. She concludes by inquiring in a nice way as to why he left her. Since the confusion hasn't touched her yet, she speaks the usual lover-language of nicely turned, somewhat formal phrases. But she won't be left in the dark for long. Or rather, the deeper darkness of the confused situation will soon descend on her, for Lysander immediately answers that he left because love made him leave. Hermia asks what love could possibly make him leave her? Lysander says his love for Helena, who illumines the night more than do the moon and stars above. He asks Hermia why she followed him-didn't she realize that he left her because he hates her? Hermia can only say that Lysander cannot be speaking his real thoughts.

Helena having heard this exchange between Lysander and Hermia, now thinks she sees what's going on: Hermia is in on the conspiracy against her. Consequently, Helena begins to reprimand Hermia for joining with Lysander and Demetrius in this "foul derision." Helena recounts all the girlhood pleasures and confidences she and Hermia have shared. She speaks of their sitting in the woods together, embroidering flowers, almost as if they were one person, so intimate was their friendship. She accuses Hermia of breaking these long-standing ties, and says she does an injury to the entire female sex in betraying her girlfriend and joining with men against her. Hermia is amazed at this outburst from Helena. To Hermia it seems that Helena scorns her, not vice versa. Helena explains more fully how things look to her. She thinks that Hermia has told Lysander to pretend that he loves Helena, and she has made her other love, Demetrius, do likewise. Why else should Demetrius, who has reviled Helena up till now, suddenly start praising and loving her? And what possible reason is there for Lysander to deny his love to Hermia except at Hermia's own instigation? Helena concludes with the self-pitying observation that since Hermia is so fortunate in love she ought to pity Helena who isn't, not despise her.

Hermia still can only say she doesn't understand what Helena means. Helena is more than ever convinced that Hermia merely pretends innocence, and she accuses them all once again of making fun of her. She says they all lack pity, grace and manners, and she'll just go away to her death somewhere. Lysander begs Helena to stay, calling her his life, his soul, his love. Helena ironically compliments his acting ability, and Hermia asks him not to scorn Helena thus. Demetrius adds his voice, saying he'll force Lysander to stop. Lysander says neither Hermia's entreaties nor Demetrius's threats can keep him from loving Helena more than life itself, and he'll lose his life to prove it. Demetrius says he loves Helena more, and he and Lysander move to fight for the proof. Hermia still asks what Lysander means by all this, and he answers, "Away, you Ethiope!" Demetrius taunts Lysander to follow and fight. Lysander shakes the clinging, loving Hermia off, and calls her a cat, a burr and a serpent. Hermia asks, "What change is this, Sweet love?" Lysander denies her: "Thy love? Out tawny Tartar, out!/Out, loathed med'cine! O hated potion, hence!" The astounded Hermia still can't believe her ears, and she inquires if Lysander is joking. Hearing this, Helena says that he is indeed joking and so is Hermia. Lysander reaffirms the challenge to fight with Demetrius, who replies that he doesn't trust Lysander, since he can't even shake Hermia off to get away for the fight. Lysander answers that even though he hates Hermia, he won't harm her. To this callous distinction, Hermia replies meaningfully. She finally begins to see that Lysander means what he says, and she observes that he can do her no greater harm than to hate her.

The word finally sinks in and she repeats it: "Hate me? Wherefore? O me, what news, my love?/ Am not I Hermia? Are you not Lysander?" She points out the obvious fact that she is as fair as ever, that just last night he loved her, and the same night he left her. Heaven forbid that he left her in earnest, Hermia concludes. Lysander says absolutely and positively yes to this question, and swears on his life as well. He says he never wanted to see her again when he left. He mercilessly pounds home the fact that he loves Helena and hates Hermia-beyond a doubt, a hope, a question, for certain, nothing truer, and no joke. At this most fierce and cruel denunciation from Lysander, Hermia turns on Helena. She calls her friend a juggler, a canker blossom, and a thief of love, who came by night and stole her Lysander's heart from her. Helena pretends to compliment Hermia on her acting ability, chides her for her brazen behavior in joking along with the men, accuses her of trying to get a rise out of Helena by pretending thus, and finally Helena calls Hermia a "counterfeit" and a "puppet." When she hears the word "puppet," Hermia thinks she begins to understand what's going on. The shorter Hermia says she now sees that Helena has won Lysander by comparing their heights, and her being taller has won him. She says Helena has grown so high in Lysander's esteem because Hermia is "so dwarfish and so low." Hermia calls Helena a "painted maypole" and says she's not too "low" to reach Helena's eyes with her nails. Helena is afraid of Hermia now, and pleads with the men to protect her, for she is very cowardly and no match for Hermia even though she is taller than Hermia.

Hermia notes this last reference to her lack of height. Helena now pleads with Hermia not to be so bitter, saying she always loved Hermia. But she adds the confession that she told Demetrius of the planned elopement in order to have his thanks and his company. Helena explains how Demetrius mistreated her in the wood, and now all she wants is to go back to Athens without any fuss, taking her foolishness with her. Hermia says that she should just leave then, who's stopping her. Helena replies that she leaves a foolish heart behind. Hermia asks if she leaves it with Lysander: Helena says she leaves it with Demetrius. Lysander tells Helena not to be afraid of Hermia, and Demetrius jumps in to be her protector too. Helena now says how fierce Hermia is when she is angry, and that she was a "vixen" at school despite her small size. Hermia is very annoyed at this repeated reference to her short stature and attempts to get to Helena. Lysander takes it upon himself to revile Hermia in particularly this way now, calling her "dwarf," "minimus," "bead," "acorn." Demetrius says Lysander meddles too much with Helena, who scorns him. Demetrius says Lysander will be sorry if he insists on demonstrating his love for Helena. Lysander says now he's free of Hermia, and he'll fight with Demetrius to see who gets Helena. Demetrius is eager to do so, and the men leave. Hermia addresses Helena now and says this whole mess is because of her. Helena backs off, saying she won't trust Hermia, nor remain in her quarrelsome company. Hermia's hands are quicker to fight, says Helena, but Helena's legs, being longer, are good for running away. Hermia can only reply, "I am amazed, and know not what to say," and both girls leave.

Comment

We have seen now the full result of Puck's mischief. The girls, who have remained constant to their original loves, bear the brunt of the confusion. Helena firmly believes the other three have joined together to make fun of her. Hermia comes to believe that Helena has won Lysander by being taller than Hermia. From their quarrel, we learn that Helena was played by a tall, light actor, and Hermia by a small, dark person. Note that at first Helena speaks of the idyllic friendship she shared with Hermia. After Hermia frightens Helena, however, the latter changes her tune: (1) She speaks of how Hermia was a vixen at school, and given to fierce outbursts. (2) Instead of just recalling their mutual trust, she now admits to having betrayed her friend's elopement to Demetrius. Hermia, from being beloved by two, is now completely unloved and unwanted. Her accusation that Helena has used her greater height to win Lysander is the foolish frenzy she is plunged into by the incomprehensible behavior of her companions. Her utter confusion is best expressed by her calling their very identities into question: "Am I not Hermia? Are you not Lysander?" she queries piteously. We cannot help but feel sorry for these tormented girls. Under the extreme pressure of these developments, the style in which the lovers speak becomes much more exciting and vivid. The men never lose their ridiculous habits-Lysander keeps swearing on his life, first one way, then the other; Demetrius is still the quintessential braggart, pompous and self-important. But note that Lysander is much more convincing in expressing his hate, much more truly passionate and feeling than when he was reciting his love to Hermia.

With all four lovers gone, Oberon addresses Puck, and lays the above havoc at his doorstep. It is Puck's negligence that is the cause, and he either made a mistake once again, or else did the mischief on purpose. Puck vows that he made a mistake. After all, he did apply the juice to someone wearing Athenian clothes as Oberon commanded. However, he freely admits that he takes great pleasure in the way things turned out - their "jangling" is a real spectator sport to him. Oberon now says that since the two men have gone off to fight, he wants Robin to make the night foggy and lead the rivals astray so they don't ever come at each other. The King tells him to imitate each man's voice, alternately stirring them up and leading them on, but always in opposite directions. Keep them thus separated till they grow very sleepy. Then, says Oberon, crush another juice on the sleeping Lysander's eyes. This second juice has the effect of removing the enchantment from his eyes so that he will love Hermia as before. Thus, Oberon continues, they will all four wake up and think all that has passed is only a "dream and fruitless vision." They will go back to Athens, correctly paired two-by-two, and remain so till death. Oberon concludes by saying that in the meantime he'll go to Titania and get the little Indian boy. Once he has this object of his desire, he'll release the Queen from the love charm, she'll no longer love the monster, and everything will be peaceful. Puck says all this must be done quickly because the dawn is approaching. He speaks of how ghosts and damned spirits who have been wandering all night must now return to their unquiet graves at crossroads or under water. They are too ashamed to have the light of day shine on them, and they willfully deny themselves daylight and only go out at night. Oberon, says, "But we are spirits of another sort." And he very beautifully describes how he has enjoyed the morning. He may stay abroad in full daylight while the red sun turns the green sea into gold. But, he concludes, let us still be quick with our business, and we'll get it done before daybreak.

Comment

Oberon here tells us how he will make everything all right. It will take time to do it, and this will be the business of the remainder of the play. Fortunately, and expectedly, the King of Fairies happens to have another juice which acts as an antidote on the first one from "the little western flower." Puck will apply this latter cure to Lysander, while Oberon himself will do the same to Titania after he has obtained the little Indian boy. We now are reminded that all this has come about because Oberon wants a changeling whom Titania has excellent reasons for wishing to keep for herself (the mother of the little boy was a dear friend who died in childbirth). Thus, despite his beautiful poetry and his kingly power, when we remember this original fact, Oberon comes off little better than the two male lovers. For magnanimity of spirit and depth of emotion, he's about on a par with them.

Puck's speech about damned spirits tells us what the spirits in this play are not like, for Oberon denies any kinship. The speech of the King in which he does this is another example of the supreme beauty that Shakespeare has given to Oberon's poetic utterances. Coming after the frenzied "jangling" (Puck's most appropriate word) of the lovers, Oberon's poetry affords us a refreshing resting-place. We lose our misgivings about his share in causing all this trouble, or rather it seems unimportant when bathed in the golden light of his poetry. After the obfuscation of the night we have been in we can only revel joyously in the morning he creates with his words.

After Oberon speaks of his delight in the morning, he leaves to find Titania. Puck remains to do his job on Lysander and Demetrius. He chants a song in happy anticipation of how he will mislead them. Then he spies Lysander, who enters searching for Demetrius. Puck speaks in Demetrius's voice and Lysander exits again in an attempt to follow the voice he has heard. Now Demetrius enters, having heard Lysander answer Puck, and demands that Lysander show himself, calling him a coward. Puck now speaks like Lysander to Demetrius and eggs him on. Demetrius cannot find his foe and now Puck says he should follow his voice and leads him away. Lysander re-enters when they have gone and complains that as fast as he follows,

Demetrius runs away even faster. He says he'll rest till daylight comes to help him find Demetrius, and he lies down and sleeps. Now Puck and Demetrius come back, and Puck is still leading Demetrius on. Demetrius dares him to wait and face up to the fight, and says he just runs away Puck continues to imitate Lysander, till finally Demetrius is exasperated with the fruitless pursuit and he too says he'll catch his foe in daylight. Then he lies down and sleeps. Now Helena enters, complaining of her weariness, and desiring daylight to come to show her the way back to Athens so she may escape the company of these that hate her. She bids sleep come to put her out of her sorrowful condition for a time. Then she goes to sleep also. Now Puck comments that one more is needed to make up the complete company - two of each kind, he says. He comments, "Cupid is a knavish lad/ Thus to make poor females mad." Now Hermia enters, weary and woebegone. She can go no further, she says, and will rest where she is till daylight. Her last words before sleeping ask that the heavens protect her Lysander if there is a fight between him and Demetrius.

Now Puck chants over Lysander and applies the curative to Lysander's eyelids. Puck's song says that when Lysander wakes he will take "True delight/ In the sight/ Of thy former lady's eye." Puck concludes his song and the scene with a country proverb: Every man should take his own. When every Jack has his Jill all will be well, predicts Puck, and with his pronouncement on life the scene closes.

SUMMARY

In this long and eventful scene, the following takes place:

(1) Puck tells Oberon how he transformed Bottom, and how Titania fell in love with him.

(2) Puck's mistaken application of the love-charm to Lysander instead of to Demetrius becomes known when Hermia is seen begging Demetrius for information on Lysander's whereabouts.

(3) To remedy the situation, Oberon enchants Demetrius and sends Puck to find Helena so that Demetrius may fall in love with her.

(4) This makes matters even worse, because now both men love Helena at once, and there is frantic quarreling and confusion when all four lovers get together.

(5) Finally, Lysander is disenchanted so that he will love Hermia again. Oberon goes to take the charm off Titania. The lovers are left sleeping and when they awake everything will be all right. They will think it was only a dream, says Oberon.

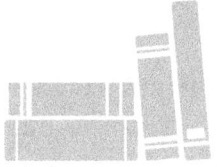

A MIDSUMMER NIGHT'S DREAM

TEXTUAL ANALYSIS

ACT 4

ACT 4: SCENE 1

We now return to the situation we left at the end of Act 3, Scene 1, where Titania is madly in love with the transformed Bottom. This scene opens with the entrance of Titania, Bottom, and the attendant fairies. Oberon is behind them. Titania is speaking lovingly to Bottom. She wants him to sit down so she can stroke his cheeks, crown him with musk-roses, and kiss his "fair large ears." Bottom, completely at home in his new environment, calls for Peaseblossom. He asks the latter to scratch his head, and then call "Monsieur Cobweb" to him and tell him to bring him some honey, adding considerately that the fairy ought to be careful not to drown in it. Bottom asks "Monsieur Mustardseed" to help "Cavalry Cobweb" scratch Bottom's head. Bottom remarks that he must go to the barber's soon, for he has an extraordinary amount of hair on his face, and he is "such a tender ass" that it tickles him. Titania asks her beloved if he would like some music, and he answers that he would like the "tongs and the bones." The Queen also inquires what he might like to eat, and Bottom replies that he wants provender, oats, and hay. Titania suggests nuts, but Bottom would rather have dried peas. What he most desires right at the moment, however, is to sleep. Titania dismisses all the fairies and, holding Bottom in her arms as the woodbine twists around the honeysuckle or as the ivy encircles the elm, they both sleep. Puck enters and Oberon advances to meet him, pointing out the sight of Titania and Bottom together. Oberon says he is beginning to pity Titania's condition. He met her while she was waiting upon Bottom and he taunted her for it. She begged his patience and he then requested the changeling, which she gave him immediately. Oberon adds the detail that the flowers with which she had crowned Bottom had dew standing in them like tears at the disgrace of being used for such a purpose. Now that Oberon has the boy, he tells Puck, he will take the charm off his Queen's eyes. He instructs Puck to remove the ass's head from Bottom so that the latter may return to Athens with everyone else. Oberon says that Bottom will think his experience to be no more than "the fierce vexation of a dream." Before Puck restores Bottom, Oberon will release Titania. Oberon recites a chant over her that says she will see with her customary eyes, and that "Dian's bud" will overpower "Cupid's flower."

Then he wakes her, and Titania says, "My Oberon, what visions have I seen!/ Methought I was enamored of an ass." Oberon points to Bottom and says she loved him. Titania wants to know how that came to be, saying she hates his sight now. Oberon asks her to be silent for awhile, he tells Puck to remove the ass's head from Bottom, and he tells Titania to call for music that will put Bottom into a deep sleep. Titania and Puck do what Oberon has bid, music plays, and the King and Queen dance hand in hand. Oberon says that he and his Queen, in renewed harmony, will dance in Theseus' house the next night and bless it. The two pairs of lovers will also be wedded in all happiness. Puck calls Oberon's attention to the sound of the morning lark. Oberon says they will leave then, adding that they can circle the world "swifter than the wand'ring moon." Titania asks that on their flight she be told how she happened to be sleeping on the ground with all we mortals. All the fairies leave.

Comment

Bottom conducts himself with propriety at the court of the Fairy Queen. The French mode of address was proper courtly behavior. His "Cavalery" is his own version of Cavalier, which is a title of address for a gallant. He is at his ease and enjoying himself. His remarks about the hair on his face are funny because he doesn't know he has an ass's head, and when he calls himself "a tender ass" he is unknowingly even funnier. The food he requests is appropriate to an ass-hay, oats, provender, dried peas. The music that he requests, though he claims to have a good ear, is not very tuneful. This is still fairyland, so flowers are mentioned: musk-roses, woodbine, honeysuckle, and ivy. Titania applies the words "amiable" and "gentle" to Bottom while she is enchanted, but in truth his behavior here warrants this praise. Though she is not herself when she says this of Bottom, Titania's description is accurate. We laugh at Bottom, but we like him too. Flowers and the moon figure in Oberon's speeches above also. Music pervades this fairy world and is part of the magic that prevails. Oberon says that Bottom will think that he has had a dream; when Titania awakens she refers to the visions that she has seen. The events of the night are thus going to pass for mere illusion with some of those who have experienced them. But Oberon can point out the real, undeniable evidence to Titania in the shape of the transformed Bottom. This should be kept in mind when the others wake up and question the reality of their experience.

Heralded by the sound of a horn, Theseus and all his attendants enter, accompanied by Hippolyta and Egeus. Theseus speaks, saying that now their performance of the May morning ritual is over and while it's still early he'll exhibit his fine hunting hounds to Hippolyta. He commands that the dogs be let loose so that she may hear the music of their barking, and he sends for the forester. The forester is the manager of game and hunting preparations in the royal forest. Theseus tells Hippolyta that they'll go up to the mountain-top to listen to the interplay of barking with echoes. She says she was with Hercules and Cadmus in Crete when they hunted a bear with Spartan hounds. She said she never heard such beautiful sounds-groves, skies, fountains, every place was filled with a concert of sound. "I never heard/ So musical a discord, such sweet thunder," Hippolyta says. Theseus is moved by this praise to claim more for his own hounds. The Duke waxes poetic in this famous description. His dogs are of the Spartan breed, and they have the same dewlaps, sandy color, long ears, and thick legs. Though slow, they are "matched in mouth like bells,/ Each under each." Theseus' enthusiasm for this latter quality leads him to say that more harmonious sounds never accompanied hunting anywhere, be it Crete, Sparta, or Thessaly, and he tells Hippolyta to decide when she hears At this moment, Theseus notices the four lovers asleep on the ground, and inquires who they are. Egeus names his daughter Hermia, Lysander, Demetrius, and Nedar's daughter Helena, and he says he wonders what they're all doing there. Theseus says they probably got up early to celebrate May Day and came to the wood because they heard the Duke was celebrating the day in the wood. Theseus asks Egeus if this is the day that Hermia is supposed to announce her choice between Demetrius as a husband on the one hand, and death or a nunnery on the other. Egeus says that it is, and Theseus orders that the huntsman wake the sleeping lovers by blowing the hunting horns. This is done, and they all start up.

Theseus greets them and makes a joke about St. Valentine's Day, when, it was thought, birds began to mate. Lysander asks the Duke's pardon. Theseus requests that they stand up, and he says he knows that the two men are rivals, so how is it that they are here together asleep? Lysander says he can only reply in amazement himself and still half-asleep, but, though he hesitates to say for certain, he thinks he came into the woods with Hermia. Yes, that was it - he came to the woods with Hermia in order to flee the Athenian law. Egeus doesn't let him get any further with his explanation. The enraged father demands the law on Lysander's head, and points out to Demetrius how Lysander was trying to cheat him. Demetrius now speaks and says Helena told him of the planned elopement. He followed them in fury, and she followed him in fancy. But, continues Demetrius, though he's at a loss to say which power, some power for sure has dissolved completely his love for Hermia, which now seems just the memory of a childhood toy. Furthermore, he is now completely enamoured of Helena, his heart belongs to Helena, he can see only Helena. Demetrius explains that he was betrothed to Helena before he loved Hermia, and he must have been like a sick man whose appetite is malfunctioning to have ever stopped loving her. Now, he's like a man returned to a healthy state who has his natural appetite again, and he loves Helena and will continue to forever. Theseus says to the lovers that their meeting was fortunate, and he'll hear more of their story later. The Duke tells Egeus that he overrides the father's wishes with respect to his daughter, and the two couples shall be married when he and Hippolyta are. Since the day has grown later, there won't be any hunting and they'll all go back to Athens for a stately feast. Theseus bids Hippolyta come and they leave with Egeus.

Comment

Hippolyta's reminiscence of a hunt with Hercules and Cadmus is not in any of the legends about Hippolyta. However, in some accounts, Theseus was a companion of Hercules in his Amazonian exploits, and hunted the Caledonian boar with other heroes. Hounds of Sparta and of Crete were celebrated breeds in antiquity. Despite the **allusions** to antiquity, the whole passage is made up of English hunting terminology. We should notice the contrast between this music, so highly praised by Theseus and Hippolyta, and the music that permeated the fairy world, to which Oberon and Titania just danced and sang before their departure a few lines before the entrance of the royal party. Of course, the coincidence of the lovers' being found by the royal party just after the fairies left them is what we have been accustomed to expect in this play. Note that the dew which bedecked flowers in the fairy world is now brushed by the long ears of bulllike hounds. Theseus is reigning in his world.

Lysander and Demetrius are vaguely aware of strange happenings and powers, but they don't know for sure. But they are finally matched to the right girlfriends, just as Oberon predicted. Of course, Demetrius is still under the effect of the love juice. We must keep this in mind when he describes how he's like a sick man returned to health now that he loves Helena again. And our awareness of this fact colors our attitude toward his proclamation of undying, permanent, perfect love for Helena. He's really still enchanted.

After Theseus, Hippolyta, and Egeus have left, the lovers remain behind for a few moments to exchange expressions of amazement at their condition. Demetrius says things seem like mountains seen at such a great distance that they look like clouds. Hermia says it's like seeing double. Helena agrees with her, and says she can't believe she really has her Demetrius-it's like finding a jewel by accident. Demetrius asks the others if they're sure they're all awake. It seems to him that he's still asleep and dreaming. He asks if the Duke came and Did them leave with him. Hermia says yes, and her father, too. Helena adds Hippolyta, and Lysander contributes that they were indeed bid to go with Theseus to the temple. Demetrius says that they must be awake then, and they ought to follow the Duke and tell each other their dreams on the way. The lovers leave.

Comment

We should note that the lovers express their confusion in terms of eyesight. Helena is accurate when she speaks of feeling as though finding Demetrius is like finding a jewel by sheer accident. She says, "Mine own, and not mine own." And we know Demetrius is still under the power of Oberon's charm. Note that Demetrius has the most to say here and he speaks of their night's experiences as "a dream."

After the lovers have left, Bottom wakes up. He thinks he's still rehearsing "Pyramus and Thisbe." His first words are that he should be summoned when his cue comes, and he gives his next cue, "Most fair Pyramus." Suddenly he wakes up enough to realize he's alone, and he calls for his companions, Quince, Flute, Snout, and Starveling. He says that they've stolen away and left him asleep, and what a "most rare vision" he's had meanwhile. Bottom's famous reaction to his experience is, "I've had a dream, past the wit of man to say what dream it was. Man is but an ass if he go about to expound this dream." Bottom begins to say what happened to him, but he breaks off and says only a fool would attempt to say what happened to him. None of man's senses can apprehend his dream, he says. In describing this, he confuses all the senses and applies them to the wrong bodily organ: the eye can't hear, the ear can't see, the hand can't taste, the tongue can't conceive, and the heart can't report what his dream was. He says he'll get Peter Quince to write a **ballad** on his dream. It will be called "Bottom's Dream" because it has no bottom, he says. He will sing it at the end of their play before the Duke, perhaps at Thisbe's death. Bottom's departure here ends the scene.

Comment

Bottom himself has told us that the profundity of his "dream" defies any comment. And indeed, his own manner of reacting to it is the best approach to the experience. Wonder, awe, and a strong sense of the power beyond man's apprehension are communicated by his words here. The confusions he commits in assigning the senses to the wrong organs are perfectly in keeping with the dramatic opposition of reality and illusion at the heart of this play. The name "Bottom's Dream" is, as he realizes, correct in both the ways he says. It is his dream, but the profundity of its implications are beyond him and he feels this power.

SUMMARY

In this scene, the following takes place:

(1) Titania is disenchanted and awakened. She is going to be told immediately what happened, and she is shown the object of her past passion right in the flesh before her.

(2) The lovers were brought to rights at the end of the last scene, but they don't know it yet. After we have seen Titania back to normal, we now return to the sleeping lovers who are awakened by Theseus. Demetrius now loves Helena, and Lysander still loves Hermia. The Duke says they'll have a triple wedding together.

(3) Last to awaken is Bottom, who rightly declares the unfathomability of his "dream" and feels most profoundly its power.

ACT 4: SCENE 2

In this scene we are back in Athens with the workmen. Quince, Flute Snout, and Starveling enter. Quince asks if anyone's been to Bottom's house to inquire if he's come home yet. Starveling says he hasn't been heard from yet, and that doubtless he's been "transported," meaning either carried off or transformed. Flute says that their play will be spoiled if he doesn't come back. They can't do it without him. Quince agrees with this, saying that no one in all Athens can play Pyramus except Bottom. Flute says Bottom has the best mind of any workman in Athens. Quince agrees and adds that Bottom has the best appearance and voice too. He uses the word "paramour" when he means "paragon" and Flute corrects him saying that a "paramour" is nothing. Snug enters with the news that the Duke has left the temple and that there are "two or three lords and ladies more married." If they had been able to perform their play it would have done them a lot of good. Flute bemoans Bottom's missing the pension the Duke surely would have granted him after seeing his marvelous performance as Pyramus. He would have deserved sixpence a day for sure. At this moment, Bottom enters, inquiring lovingly for his friends. He calls them "lads" and "hearts." Quince exclaims with joy and calls the day "courageous" and the hour "most happy." Bottom tells his friends that he'll tell them wonders, but they mustn't ask what. Then he says he'll tell them everything just as it happened. Quince asks to hear. Now Bottom won't say a word, except that the Duke is through dinner, and they must get ready to perform their play. He instructs them to be clean and well-groomed, except for the lion's long nails, and not to eat onions or garlic. Thus they'll have sweet breath and their play will be considered a sweet comedy. He bids them depart without further talk and they all leave.

Comment

We should note that this scene, and Bottom's speech at the end of the last scene, are in prose. These characters always speak in prose. The conversation before Bottom arrives exhibits the great concern and affection Bottom's friends have for him. His first words to them show that this is mutual. Bottom seems to be about to tell his friends about the experience he has had, but for now anyway, he just can't. All immediate interest is turned toward the play to be presented before the Duke.

SUMMARY

The purpose of this short scene is to show Bottom's return to normal. Although the scene is very brief, we do learn some important things:

(1) Bottom is loved and admired both his friends and they are very sad at his strange disappearance. Their remarks convey warm and true feeling. They may not be gentlemen, but they are gentle, simple men with admirable qualities.

(2) Bottom returns to them warm and real as always. His first words are full of the special quality that is Bottom: "Where are these lads? where are these hearts?" Direct, energetic, and above all loving, he takes charge with his accustomed vigor and enthusiasm.

(3) Finally, we learn that their play of "Pyramus and Thisbe" has been selected as the evening's entertainment at court where several more people have been married. It really doesn't matter how many (Snug says two or three more couples), for as Flute points out, "a paramour is, God bless us, a thing of naught." From what we have seen in the moonlight of the mad wood, this point of view seems right enough.

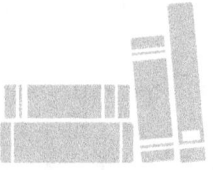

A MIDSUMMER NIGHT'S DREAM

TEXTUAL ANALYSIS

ACT 5

ACT 5: SCENE 1

In this scene we are back in Theseus' palace again. Theseus, Hippolyta, Philostrate, Lords, and Attendants enter. Hippolyta remarks that what the lovers have spoken of is strange. Theseus answers in a famous speech about the lover, the madman and the poet. He says the lovers' story is "more strange than true," and he for one never believes old stories and fairy tales. Lovers and madmen have "seething brains" that grasp more than reason can understand. In fact, he continues, the lunatic, the lover, and the poet all have the same kind of imagination, they just imagine different things. The madman sees more devils than there are in hell. The equally frantic lover imagines a mere gypsy to be as beautiful as Helen of Troy. The frenzied eye of the poet looks back and forth between heaven and earth and whatever the imagination comes up with, he with his pen gives a shape and a name to it. In Theseus' famous words, the poet "gives to airy nothing/ A local habitation and a name." He says the imagination has such "tricks" that if it wants to grasp a joy, it can use reason to understand how to bring that joy. Theseus concludes with the example of being frightened at night and thinking that a bush is a bear.

However, Hippolyta still says that the whole story, with everyone's minds "transfigured so together," is more than fanciful imaginings. The story exhibits great constancy, even though it is strange and admirable. Theseus says that the lovers are coming, mirthful and joyous. At this point, Lysander, Demetrius, Hermia, and Helena enter, and Theseus wishes them joy and love. Lysander replies with the wish that the Duke have even more of the same. Theseus asks what entertainment is available to pass the time away between after-supper and bedtime. He calls for Philostrate, the manager of entertainment at court, and the latter says that he is here. Theseus asks him what entertainment is available and Philostrate hands him a list of possibilities which the Duke reads out loud. Out of four choices he selects "Pyramus and Thisbe" and questions Philostrate about it. The description given him interests him by its strange combinations: "A tedious brief scene of young Pyramus/ And his love Thisbe; very tragical mirth" is what the tradesmen have called their offering. Theseus comments on the combination of opposites. Philostrate explains that though the play is very short indeed, it is tedious to watch because it is performed so badly; and though Pyramus kills himself, the whole performance made Philostrate laugh.

Theseus asks who the players are and is told about the efforts of the Athenian workmen who are rank amateurs completely unaccustomed to using their minds. Theseus says he wants to see the play. Philostrate tries to dissuade him, saying the only thing amusing about it is how hard they try. But Theseus insists on his choice, saying that if their intentions are good that's all that counts, and he sends Philostrate to get the performers. Hippolyta says she doesn't want to watch these workmen struggle and fail to please. Theseus says she needn't worry, and she replies that Philostrate said they were completely inept. Theseus says that, in that case, more kindness and nobility will be required of the audience. He tells her how he is often confronted with tongue-tied public officials and yet he knows that they mean well. Philostrate comes back and says that the Prologue of the play is ready to be spoken. Quince speaks his part and he doesn't punctuate and pause meaningfully, so it comes out all wrong. Theseus, Lysander, and Hippolyta remark how little sense his speech made. Each has a different **metaphor** for this. Next enter the rest of the actors: Pyramus, Thisbe, Wall, Moonshine, and Lion. Quince continues with the prologue and gives a summary of the story and introduces each character. They all leave except Wall. Theseus says he wonders if the lion will speak and Demetrius makes the joke that one lion may, since many asses do. Now Wall speaks and introduces himself as Snout, telling what his part is in the play. Through a chink in this wall the lovers whisper. Theseus and Demetrius remark on the wit of the wall in speaking so. Now Pyramus re-enters, and addresses the black night and the wall, asking where is his Thisbe. He looks through the chink and cannot see her. Theseus says the wall should answer, but Bottom tells him that's not the way the play goes. It is Thisbe's cue and she will enter in a moment, he patiently explains.

Thisbe enters and addresses her love-complaint to the wall that always separates her from Pyramus. Pyramus says that he "sees" her voice and he'll try to "hear" her face. The lovers then greet each other and liken their love to that of famous lovers in the past, only they make their usual errors in doing it. Instead of "Leander and Hero" they mention "Limander and Helen" and for "Cephalus" and "Procris" they say "Shafalus" and "Procrus."

This loving exchange is in the form of single, alternating lines of dialogue, rhymed by twos ("stichomythia"). Pyramus and Thisbe arrange to meet at "Ninny's tomb" and Pyramus says he'll be there, come life or death. They exit, and so does Wall, after first saying that he's done his job so he's leaving. Theseus, Demetrius, and Hippolyta exchange comments on what they have just seen. They think it's silly and Theseus says all acting is just "shadows" requiring the audience to use imagination. For this performance, one has to use a little more imagination, that's all. Lion and Moonshine re-enter now, and Lion explains that he's really Snug the joiner so the ladies won't be frightened. Theseus, Demetrius, and Lysander must comment here too, and they exchange supercilious witticisms about the discretion and valor of Lion. Now Moonshine tries to explain his characterization, but Demetrius and Theseus persist in their disruptive comments. Their joke is that old stand-by about horns, since Moonshine says he is the "horned" (crescent) moon. Hippolyta says she is weary of the moon and wishes it would change. Theseus makes another comment and finally Moonshine gets to speak his whole speech.

But as soon as he finishes, Demetrius must unnecessarily point out that all the objects that Starveling is carrying ought to be inside the lantern since they are inside the moon. Now Thisbe re-enters to keep her appointment at "Ninny's tomb" and she is frightened away by the roar of Lion. Demetrius, Theseus, and Hippolyta compliment Lion, Thisbe and Moon. Hippolyta had said she was weary of the moon, but here she says, "Truly, the moon shines with a good grace." The Lion now shakes the mantle Thisbe dropped before he exits. Theseus, Lysander and Demetrius comment briefly. Pyramus comes in now and, seeing the blood-stained mantle of Thisbe, recites a passionate speech. Theseus says it almost makes a man sad to see this. Hippolyta remarks feelingly, "Beshrew my heart, but

I pity the man." Pyramus continues his passionate expression of grief and concludes by killing himself. Moonshine exits and Pyramus dies. Demetrius, Lysander, and Theseus comment once again. Hippolyta inquires how Thisbe will find her lover with the moon gone, and Theseus replies that she will find him by starlight. Thisbe re-enters and Hippolyta says that she hopes she'll be brief. Demetrius and Lysander also comment. Thisbe finds Pyramus and, after first thinking he's asleep, she sorrows deeply over his death. She describes him as having the colors of various flowers: "lily lips," "cherry nose," "yellow cowslip cheeks," and eyes "green as leeks." She calls on the Fates who have killed him to end her life, and she stabs herself to death. Theseus says that Moonshine and Lion are now left to bury the dead lovers. Demetrius adds Wall. At this, Bottom starts up and explains that the wall of hostility between their two families is now no longer. He asks if the audience wishes to see an epilogue or to hear a dance.

Theseus says no epilogue is needed and compliments them on the performance. He requests that they perform their dance instead. Afterwards, the Duke announces that it is midnight and time for bed. It's almost "fairy time" says Theseus and he's afraid they'll oversleep the next morning from being up so late. The performance of "Pyramus and Thisbe" has made the evening pass very quickly. He concludes by saying that they'll continue to celebrate for another fortnight (two weeks), and with these words, everyone leaves.

Comment

Duke Theseus' speech about the lover, madman, and poet expresses the view of the practical, successful man of affairs. He does his public job very well, is a brave soldier and a trustworthy leader. However, the wondrous realms of art and love are to him as unapproachable as madness. Hippolyta is more open than he and she feels the power of these other realms.

Having the performance of a play take place within the larger play as a whole allows Shakespeare to show us the reactions of those characters who witness it. That is the case here, and while Lysander and Demetrius are joking at the expense of the earnest tradesmen, we should remember how absurdly they behaved in the woods. Demetrius does most of the disruptive jesting, and it is he who still has the love juice on his eyes that causes him to love Helena. Notice that Helena and Hermia, who have been constant to their loves, do not engage in the jesting aimed at the workmen's performance.

When everyone has left, Puck enters. He describes the night - the wild animals that roar, howl, and screech; the ghosts that leave their graves to wander abroad; and the fairies like himself that "follow darkness like a dream," and at night make merry. He says nothing shall disturb Theseus' house, and he has been sent with a broom to sweep there. Oberon and Titania enter with their attendants, and the fairies sing and dance. Oberon bids his subjects go about the house blessing everyone. He himself will bless the royal union so that they shall love forever and have perfect offspring. He hands out "field-dew" to be sprinkled in blessing everywhere, and instructs everyone to meet at daybreak. The King and Queen leave with their followers. Puck has the last words in the play. He says that if the play has not pleased but offended, just write it off as a dream. If they're lucky enough to escape being hissed and booed, then he promises they'll improve. And if the audience applauds, then Puck will do good for them. With this, the spirit exits and the play ends.

Comment

We have seen Snug play a lion, and when Puck enters he describes the real night inhabited by fierce animals and frightening sounds. He speaks of cleaning the palace because Puck is traditionally represented as having a broom and cleaning the houses of those whom he favored. Oberon speaks of preventing disfigured children because folklore ascribed this power to fairies. We should note that once again dew is mentioned. It is fitting that Puck should have the last word, and that he suggest to us the possibility of the whole play's being only a dream. This has been "A Midsummer Night's Dream."

SUMMARY

In the last scene of the play the following is accomplished:

(1) All the lovers have been married to the right persons.

(2) The workmen perform at court the play they have prepared for this purpose.

(3) The fairies enter when all else is done and bless all with peace and prosperity.

Thus, all strands are woven together harmoniously.

A MIDSUMMER NIGHT'S DREAM

CHARACTER ANALYSES

Theseus

A just ruler and a brave warrior, Theseus embodies the virtues of the public man of action. He speaks with the voice of honest and trustworthy authority. His tastes and opinions are those of a man trained in the arts of war and government. Despite all these positive qualities, Theseus lacks the finer sensibilities. The scope of his vision is markedly limited to those realms in which he is accustomed to move with authority, understanding all that he sees and always in control of the situation. Thus his pronouncements within the play express a limited point of view. He is forever shut out from the beauty and mystery of love and dreams and art, for all are illusion and madness to him. The lover, the madman, and the pert are all excluded from his world of "cool reason." Imagination is suspect. He sees it as a disorder that is opposed to the order he believes in of just politics and heroic war. The beauty he enjoys is the music of his hunting dogs whose barking ordered along the scale wins his admiration and praise. But Theseus is deaf to the music of the moonlit woods.

Hippolyta

As ruler and warrior in her own right, Hippolyta shares some of the above characteristics with Theseus. However, she has a natural sympathy and warmth that moderates these qualities. This is seen by her refusal to discount completely the stories the lovers tell as mere nonsense the way Theseus does. She is also very concerned for the well-being of the workmen, and she is quite moved by Pyramus's passion. She is much less fully portrayed than Theseus, but we are given evidence that her womanly qualities temper her attitude, and though she is the female counterpart of the Duke she differs from him insofar as this is true.

Lysander

We are meant to see Lysander as a rather typical young man, and indeed there is little to differentiate him as a character. Our main means of remembering him is that he is the one whom Hermia loves in return. The forcefulness of his intent to elope with his beloved is marred by his inability to carry it through- he gets lost on the way. His formal declarations of undying love suffer from being made to two different girls. The most sincere expressions would crumble under that blow and Lysander's words are weak to begin with. But it is unseemly to judge him harshly. He is just meant to be another young man in love, and to expect more is to ask for an altogether different character.

Demetrius

The point about Demetrius is that he is so little different from Lysander, and vice versa. In fact, they even love the same girl at the beginning of the play. And as was said of Lysander, Hermia's action makes all the difference between them. She chooses Lysander, and that imposes Demetrius's role on him. The only other distinguishing mark is his abandonment of Helena, but Lysander's later denial of Hermia blurs this distinction also. Actually, it is Helena's constant and faithful love for Demetrius which serves mainly to distinguish him as a character. However, Demetrius does have the dubious distinction of being the one character in the play who remains enchanted. Thus when he is so loudmouthed in his superior scorn of the "Pyramus and Thisbe" play, we do notice him especially. We think, who is he to mock this earnest endeavor as foolish, and this questioning of his identity is our primary reaction to him as a character.

Hermia

At first Hermia is the typical young girl in love against her father's wishes. Perhaps we have a slight clue that a real person lies behind this stock exterior when she promises to meet Lysander "By all the vows that ever men have broke/ (In number more than ever women spoke)." This remark has life and reality, especially in the light of what follows. In itself, too, it has a spark of originality-she could have just sworn on her life the way Lysander is always doing. When the play has progressed to the height of love's confusion, Hermia emerges as very distinct indeed. She is dark and small, but quick-tempered even to fierceness. Though she and Helena may once have been almost two persons in one body as they sat in girlish companionship, under the pressure of being a woman bereft of her man this twinship is sundered and each girl emerges as a separate personality. Driven almost to madness by Lysander's unaccountable rejection of her, Hermia asks exactly the right question, "Am not I Hermia? are not you Lysander?'

The men, who are not in control at all, keep avowing their new-found sanity and sobriety. But Hermia, who remains constant throughout, sees her very identity at stake. Her awareness of this question is itself an assertion of her identity so that when she gets her Lysander back she gets more than just that. She gets herself back too in an increased way by having felt the basis of her identity threatened. Hermia does not say anything during the performance of the play. In fact, her last words are in Act 4, Scene 1, when she says she feels as if she were seeing double. One cannot say for sure, but perhaps Hermia's silence in the rest of the play indicates that the experience she had in the wood did have a permanent, beneficial effect. Perhaps Shakespeare is telling us by this that she knows better now than to do as Lysander and Demetrius do. But this must remain a conjecture, for the fabric of the play will not support weighty contentions. Puck makes certain that the gossamer veil remains between us and all that has passed before us on the stage-he says to consider it all a dream. And behind the sheer gossamer, everything shimmers brightly, but it perforce remains tantalizingly indistinct.

Helena

Helena is the love-sick, love-lorn maiden. She is tall and fair, and until events conspire against her, she droops and pines beautifully all over her cruel beloved. She does show some measure of initiative when she betrays her best friend so that she can gain her own ends with her boy friend. And her persistent, abject humility is certainly remarkable. When she suddenly finds herself beloved of two instead of by none, she is forced out of her accustomed role. She is full of self-pity at this discomfort-she's much more adept at being love-lorn through long habit. Perhaps she sees herself as quite pretty at pining and pleading, pale and slender as she is. Anyway, her immediate reaction is to suspect a plot, and she pities herself all the more. Her chief defense is that her plight deserves pity, not scorn. This attitude remains intact for a time. She deploys it artfully to upbraid Hermia, saying that the latter shamefully betrays their long and fast friendship. How can Hermia be so cruel to such a sweet, dear, faithful, trusting friend, and one who has had such a hard time of it already? But when Hermia's temper flares, things look a little different. Now Helena remembers an action a little at variance with the earlier idyllic portrayal of her relationship with Hermia. In fact, she confesses that she betrayed her friend's confidence and told the person who would most like to spoil the elopement all about it. A little later it is revealed by the frightened Helena that things weren't so rosy back in the good old days either. In fact, Helena's opinion is that Hermia was a fierce vixen at school.

So, under pressure Helena ventures out a little more on her own too. She actually gathers her dropping, love-sick self together enough to run away from Hermia. Fear of bodily harm from her little friend replaces the piteous sorrow with which she withstood all manner of threats from Demetrius. This abandonment of her initial role is a step forward toward an individual personality. Running from Hermia interests us much more than her running after Demetrius. Helena, too, says no more after Act 4, Scene 1, and her comment there is quite perceptive. She says she can't feel secure about Demetrius-it's like finding a jewel by lucky accident. We who know Demetrius's true state couldn't have said it any better. And so, though we must leave this as mere conjecture for the same reason as we did for Hermia, we can't deny that somehow Helena knows what she's getting when she gets Demetrius.

Egeus

The father of Hermia, Egeus is the typical disgruntled father whose daughter is silly enough to love whom she wants, not whom he wants. The first words we hear him speak establish him as this kind of character. He says he's "full of vexation" at Hermia, and the reasons he gives are the typical response of the older, stolid generation to young and wayward love. Egeus is a man to whom the accoutrements of love are just stuff and nonsense. Balconies by moonlight, love poetry, souvenirs, gifts of jewelry, flowers, and candy are all a silly nuisance in his opinion. All they do is interfere with the orderly, business-like fulfillment by a dutiful daughter of a marriage contract made by a responsible father. Egeus is the embodiment of this classic attitude toward love and marriage. He would rather see his daughter dead or shut up in a nunnery than married to someone he hasn't chosen for her.

Bottom

Nick Bottom the weaver is one of Shakespeare's most memorable creations. When we first meet him, the play of "Pyramus and Thisbe" is being cast. Bottom is ready to take on anything. He has complete confidence in his ability to sweep from one end of the emotional scale to the other. The energy and enthusiasm with which he participates in life are immediately evident. Some critics have objected to what they consider his domineering, brash, self-centered personality, but this is a gross misunderstanding. When he shares Titania's bower, his easy graciousness with his extraordinary new companions is a mark of his marvelous ability to adapt immediately to whatever life offers him. His energetic love of life, his naiveté and eager innocence obtain his entrance into this other-world so different from his own.

And he enjoys it to the fullest. When Bottom awakens from his "dream," his own manner of reacting to it is the best approach to the experience. Wonder, awe, and a strong sense of the power beyond man's apprehension are communicated by his words there. He rightly declares the unfathomability of his "dream" and feels most profoundly its power. He knows that it should be called "Bottom's Dream" for these correct reasons. Starting from his position as a rock-bottom realist, Bottom can, with the same vigor and joy he brings to whatever he does, respond to this power and believe.

The fantastically transformed Bottom, seemingly the least likely candidate in all the world before his transformation, becomes a participator in the fairy world in the incredible role of Titania's beloved. But we see thus that it was possible after all; indeed it seems an absolutely necessary liaison once we see how naturally Bottom takes it. He conducts himself with such sobriety and yet such grace, with his own good sense and yet with such enjoyment that we see he is a weaver in this deeper sense too-Bottom the weaver is supremely capable of uniting these disparate worlds. His very person embodies the union of reality and illusion, carrying as he does Puck's trick on his real, sturdy shoulders. His love of life enables him to engage in it to the fullest. The fullness of his engagement unites experience. In this play where love and art and dreams assert their power over life, Bottom embodies the union of reality and illusion wherein lie the secret springs and mysterious force of life itself.

Peter Quince, Francis Flute, Tom Snout, Snug, Robin Starveling

These worthy, simple men pursue various trades in Athens. Quince is a carpenter, Snout is a tinker, Flute is a bellows-mender, Snug is a joiner, Starveling is a tailor. They are Bottom's companions and together with him they prepare and present the play of "Pyramus and Thisbe" as a wedding entertainment at Theseus' and the lovers' marriages. We laugh at these "hempen homespuns" (as Puck calls them), at their blunders with language, and at their inept theatrical venture. But we are shown that they love Bottom and he loves them. We feel the warmth and reality of these characters and admire their simple earnestness. They are far less foolish than those who mock them as fools. And they perform the valuable service in this play of highlighting this last fact.

Oberon

The King of the Fairies has the majesty and power in his world that Theseus has in his. The difference between the two worlds bespeaks the difference between the two characters, for Oberon is triumphant in poetry and illusion - "King of Shadows" Puck calls him, while as mere shadows Theseus disparages even the most expert purveyors of illusion (Act 5, Scene 1, lines 212 and 213). The marriage of Theseus is the framing event in the daylight world of the play. It is the first thing we hear of and the last thing that happens, but the cloth that is woven within this frame is of Oberon's design. He and his assistant Puck move the shuttle of this loom madly between the straight uprights of Theseus' frame. The lovers are matched as warp and woof, and Bottom's experience runs as a strong diagonal thread knitting all sturdily.

All this comes about because Oberon can't have something that he wants. Titania has a changeling whom she has excellent reasons for wishing to keep. The little boy's mother was a special friend who died giving birth to this child. But Oberon must have this boy. He obtains the love juice to divert Titania's interest from the child and he'll only disenchant her once the changeling is securely in his own train. When we remember that this is the motive behind all that happens in the woods, Oberon comes off little better than the two male lovers. For magnanimity of spirit and depth of emotion he's about on a par with them. However, as soon as Oberon speaks the poetry Shakespeare has given him, we too are completely in his power. His magnificent description of the occasion when he first saw "the little western flower" obliterates any lingering doubts about the petty purpose he intends it for. His poetry evokes a music that made "the rude sea" grow civil and caused the stars to shoot "madly from their spheres." This is the Oberon we remember, the King of Shadows to whom such things happen and who can thus recreate his experiences.

Titania

The Queen of Fairies carries herself with the nobility and dignity befitting her station. When Oberon tries to bully her into giving up her changeling, she stands up to him with admirable spirit and we feel she has the right on her side. But the action which does most to create her as a character in our eyes is of a very different nature. Charmed by the love juice, Titania coddles and caresses Bottom. This appears highly ridiculous to Oberon and Puck, but somehow it increases her stature in our eyes. We can't help but like her better for it. First, we have affection for Bottom and he reacts beautifully to his new and completely foreign situation. In addition, Titania does not lower herself-she treats him well and wants to make him a pure spirit like herself. The effect of all this is that though she is the female counterpart of Oberon in many ways, the woman in her also plays a part in our conception of her character.

Puck

This mischievous elf is unique unto himself. There is no way to describe him, except in his own words. He tells us he loves preposterous things best and he delights no end in the pranks he executes in this play. He is a homey, rustic spirit. His language and the kind of mischief he specializes in demonstrate this. Though Oberon is his master, Puck is immediately responsible for the confusions. It is he who mistakes Lysander for Demetrius and puts the ass's head on Bottom. And it is also he who suggests to us that perhaps the whole play is nothing but a dream.

Peaseblossom, Cobweb, Moth, Mustardseed

The fairies in *A Midsummer Night's Dream* are Shakespeare's invention. There had, of course, been fairies in English folklore, but Shakespeare's differ in several important respects from these. It is Shakespeare's fairies as depicted in this play which have held sway over the public imagination ever since their creation, replacing those of folk tradition. Shakespeare's differ from the latter in three outstanding ways: their diminutive size, their association with flowers, and their benevolent natures. The fairy of folklore had none of these characteristics. The popular conception that has prevailed has them because it is derived from Shakespeare's creation in this play. The names of the above fairies in particular are in keeping with the tiny, airy, delicate creatures Shakespeare has created. The activities that Titania assigns to them paint an extraordinary scene of the whimsical, delightful, non-mortal world that is brought into being in this play.

Philostrate

This minor character is in charge of providing entertainment at Duke Theseus' court. All we know about him is that he thinks the workmen's play is unworthy to be seen, and say it is "nothing, nothing in the world." Of course, we know that there are lots of things outside of this world inhabited by Philostrate. Puck, for instance, who in another world is a very different "master of revels." Theseus sent Philostrate out to prepare entertainment at the very beginning, just as Oberon sent Puck to fetch the love juice. The difference between the two lieutenants is in keeping with the difference between the two masters. Philostrate is not characterized at all fully, but he does serve to complete a certain pleasing symmetry.

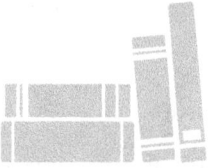

A MIDSUMMER NIGHT'S DREAM

CRITICAL COMMENTARY

A Midsummer Night's Dream was performed for James I on January 1, 1604. During the 17th century it went through several revivals and revisions; one for an actor named Tawyer whose name appears on the script, one in 1631 for a bishop. There were versions of the play in 1661 and 1672. Apparently, the play was performed as a "droll" or clown play, for the title in 1661 was *The Merry Conceited Humors of Bottom the Weaver*. Samuel Pepys records having seen our play, but from his manner of dismissing it as mere nonsensical frivolity we suspect that he saw a doctored version. The 17th century diarist is not specific enough for us to know whether he saw Shakespeare's original version or not.

The sobriety of the 18th century would not take kindly to *A Midsummer Night's Dream*, one would expect. In fact, from the title of Garrick's *The Fairies* (published 1755), we suspect extensive revamping. The 18th century was an age of great editors of Shakespeare. Pope, Rowe, Theobald, Hanmer, Warburton, and Dr. Johnson edited editions of the plays. There are four phases to the 18th-century interest in Shakespeare: (1) Scholars deal with Shakespeare's neglect of the so-called rules of drama (actually incorrectly derived from Aristotle's *Poetics*); (2) There is an attempt to determine the extent of his learning; (3) The treatment of the text is a major preoccupation of this period; (4) There begins to be an interest in Shakespeare as a delineator of character. The venerable Dr. Johnson says that *A Midsummer Night's Dream*, along with *The Tempest*, were the noblest efforts of a sublime and amazing imagination peculiar to Shakespeare. He thinks that the scene where the workmen are cast in their play shows Shakespeare ridiculing the prejudices and the competition of players. He suggests emendations in the text and wonders why the play is called *A Midsummer Night's Dream*, since we are informed it happened on May Day. This last point is much argued by German critics of this period and later. It will be dealt with definitively by one of the recent critics below.

Johnson says the play is well-written in its various modes and gives the pleasure the author intended. Of the fairies he says they were much in fashion in Shakespeare's time-common tradition had made them familiar and Spenser's poem (*The Fairy Queen*) had made them great. We will see in a more recent study below that Johnson fails to make the necessary distinction between Shakespeare's fairies and those of popular tradition. In fact, fairies like those in this play were not in fashion till Shakespeare's play made them so. This matter shall be dealt with more extensively when we speak of the book on this subject below.

In the early 19th century Shakespeare criticism reached new heights. Critics such as Samuel Taylor Coleridge, William Hazlitt, and Charles Lamb turned perceptive intelligences and impassioned rhetoric to the service of exalting "The Bard." "Bardolotry" has been coined as a term to denote the reverence in which he was held. The emphasis was on character analysis and the tragedies came in for close inspection on this level. A play like *A Midsummer Night's Dream* was less fertile ground for such speculations, especially since it was commonly performed in butchered versions on the order of light, comic, music-hall operettas. This elicited Hazlitt's disapproval and in his critical remarks he bemoans the distortions of such a production. Hazlitt is very perceptive in his remarks on *A Midsummer Night's Dream* when he speaks of how perfectly the name and trade of each workman go together. Yet this is done so subtly, says Hazlitt, that we feel it is natural - these are real men with real names. Late 19th century character analysis culminates in a classic of Shakespearean criticism: A. C. Bradley's *Shakespearean Tragedy*. Our play is obviously not dealt with in this book, but its great influence on all criticism of Shakespeare cannot be overlooked even here.

The 20th-century critics of Shakespeare have come to pay more and more attention to the comedies, which used to be considered unanalyzable. However, there is no clear line of development in the critical approaches taken. Single plays and special aspects are dealt with, but until very recently, there has been no effort to follow through to a comprehensive statement. Generally speaking, there has been much detailed work and little concentrated effort. John Russell Brown, in his survey of the situation from 1900-1953, establishes the following categories of critical work on the comedies: (1) literary influences; (2) sources; (3) Elizabethan stage, life, and thought; (4) character, **theme**, language.

H. B. Charlton in his *Shakespearean Comedy* (1938) discusses the purpose and **theme** of Shakespeare's comedies by tracing the evolution of these plays from the forms of English, Italian, and classical comedy. J. R. Brown points out in his survey that individual examination might not have disclosed this. Charlton devotes a whole chapter in his book to *A Midsummer Night's Dream*, in which he says the play deals with the contemporary love question and is weak in characterization. His formulation of the contemporary love question is that for an Elizabethan, to live was to love, and that, romantically. He says that the question underlying the play is, What is the place of love in life? Charlton points out that the pansy, or "little western flower," indicates that the spell of love was in the English countryside. This prepares the world for poets and lovers who are fairy-ridden and liable to love. In this play, he continues, the poet's world of fairies and the lovers' rural England are one. People must love and love is a power and does not involve reason. Charlton closes his remarks on *A Midsummer Night's Dream* with a discussion of Bottom. In this critic's opinion, Bottom incarnates the theory of Theseus, which Charlton understands as stating that men will never be allowed out of touch with earth. Charlton concludes by saying that Theseus' cool reason is the philosophy of comedy and the prevailing spirit for success in the world. Shakespeare is advocating unromantic worldly **realism**, Charlton believes, not classical romance. As opposed to the latter, Shakespearean romance has as its aim the preservation of the whole race.

T. M. Parrott, in his *Shakespearean Comedy* (1949), sketches the main outlines of literary influences and deals with Shakespeare's sources. Of *A Midsummer Night's Dream* he says that the central action is concerned with that phase of human love called "fancy" by the Elizabethans - the irrational impulse that draws man to maid and maid to man. O. J. Campbell worked with the source question on Love's *Labour's Lost and on Two Gentlemen of Verona*, showing that certain details were derived from the dramatist Lyly rather than from Italian dramas. He deals with *A Midsummer Night's Dream* in terms of the three groups: fairies, mortals, and workmen. He says the first is a vehicle for contemporary political **satire** and comment. Of the second he says it is Italianate and has slightly delineated characters. With respect to the third, he speaks of Bottom as portraying absurd humanity. Campbell gives the wedding of Derby and Vere on January 26, 1595, as the occasion of the play. (Refer to Introduction for discussion of this.)

Northrop Frye discusses the comedies in terms of basic types of character, social reconciliation, and the debt to folk plays and rituals. This critic uses the concept of the "drama of the green world" to link the early to the late plays. The critics Israel Gollancz and Muriel Bradbrook concern themselves with the medieval sources of Shakespeare's comedies. Nevill Coghill also contributes to this phase of Shakespeare studies.

M. W. Latham, in The *Elizabethan Fairies* (1930), establishes the fact that Shakespeare created his own fairies in *A Midsummer Night's Dream*. This critic's thorough investigation reveals the following changes made by Shakespeare so that his fairies differ from those of popular folk tradition:

(1) These fairies are not members of a powerful commonwealth with its own rulers, but attendants on two literary or mythical sovereigns.

(2) They are benevolent creatures.

(3) Robin Goodfellow (Puck) is introduced to emphasize the difference between these fairies and the traditional ones.

(4) These spirits are thoroughly associated with flowers.

(5) Their reduction in size to diminutive is an invention of Shakespeare that furthers the comedy.

To summarize, their dignity is diminished, their size is reduced, their character is redeemed, and they are associated with flowers and insects-all of which makes them a new race of spirits. Latham also devotes a chapter of this book to Robin Goodfellow, pointing out that he is differentiated from the fairies, though a member of that world in this play. Not before was he a fairy or a puck (devil).

G. Wilson Knight, in his *The Shakespearean Tempest* (1932), deals with **imagery**, verse, and style. He looks for "poetic color and suggestion" above all. This stimulating critic has taught others to look for implicit value judgments in passages previously thought merely poetic or descriptive. Thus he shows the way to a new view of thematic unity and coherence in the comedies. John Crowe Ransom, in the *Kenyon Review* (1947), deals with Oberon's speech about Titania's bower. He puts forth psychological explanations for our reaction to this kind of poetry. D. L. Stevenson, in his *The Love-game Comedy* (1946), discusses the **theme** of courtship in several early comedies, not including our play.

Also in 1946 appeared John Palmer's *Comic Characters of Shakespeare*, in which the critic discusses Berowne, Touchstone, Shylock, Bottom, and Beatrice and Benedick. This critic's remarks on Bottom are excellent. He points out how Bottom holds the play together and is an "immortal weaver," having a genius for accommodation with all things within the limits of his imaginable world. Palmer says this play is Bottom's dream from first to last. Bottom is like Shakespeare-if he come not, the play is marred. Bottom takes us along with him by virtue of the same quality that allowed Shakespeare to go inside a fairy or a Hamlet. This quality is that genius for accommodation that both have.

Two recent books deal with *A Midsummer Night's Dream* in important ways. John Russell Brown's *Shakespeare and His Comedies* (1957) discusses the significance of the play within the play. Brown states that Shakespeare saw in the relationship of actor, audience, and drama the image of man's recognition of imagined truths. In this book there is a valuable discussion of the use of the play within the play elsewhere in Shakespeare. This critic attempts a comprehensive view of the comedies and in his conclusion he states that the three main **themes** he has discussed (love's wealth, love's truth, and love's order) form a developing and comprehensive view of love, personal relationships, and of life as experienced through such relationships.

Another recent study (C. L. Barber's *Shakespeare's Festive Comedy*, 1959) explores the way the social form of Elizabethan holidays contributed to the dramatic form of festive comedy. This critic is interested in how art develops the underlying configurations in the social life of a culture. In his chapter on *A Midsummer Night's Dream*, Barber points out that the May game gave the pattern for the whole action, which moves "from the town to the grove" and back again, "bringing in summer to the Bridal." He says that the pattern of the May game was so familiar that it needn't be mentioned in the title of the play. "Through release to clarification" is the pattern of such festivities. With Barber's study we are returned, answer in hand, to the question Dr. Johnson of the 18th century could not resolve. The later critic explains that May games were a type of activity that could take place at other times such as midsummer.

A MIDSUMMER NIGHT'S DREAM

ESSAY QUESTIONS AND ANSWERS

Question: Discuss the three worlds of the play. Be specific in your examples.

Answer: The four lovers inhabit one of the worlds of the play. Their situation is that of a stock thwarted romance, with the father demanding his daughter marry a man she doesn't love. The situation also includes a lovelorn maiden who has been abandoned by this same man. Although this situation contains the ingredients of tragedy, we see that the treatment is decidedly in a lighter, comic vein. Rather than a display of great passion and emotional strife, the speeches made are so stylized and formal that what we observe are the typical young lovers in the typical thwarted romance. We are meant to respond this way and are kept thus from feeling the deeper, stronger, more tragic emotions that are potentially present. A very formal verse form, stichomythia, is employed in two places by the lovers. When the confusion is at its height in the woods, they do break out of their customary wooden mode and exhibit some true feeling. This is more true of the girls than of their boy friends, who persist in a rather shallow, trifling vein.

Another world in this play is occupied by the Athenian workmen. These characters are very, very different from the above. In contrast to the formal poetry that the lovers speak, these amiable simple men speak the prose of comic **realism**. Their situation is also markedly contrasted. The lovers become deluded and misled by illusion in the form of Puck's mischief with the love juice. The workmen undertake to deal with illusion in the form of a play they produce for Theseus' wedding. We are shown their rehearsal, which displays the great pains they take to explain away every illusion. To these men, reality and illusion are two entirely separate entities, and they insist upon stating which is which at every point where the slightest confusion might arise. They take absolutely no chances on this question. The manner in which their production goes forward is a classic expression of the position they represent on the reality-illusion question - a question at the heart of this play. When Bottom and his fellows deal with the moon, even that evanescent, inconstant body is brought down to earth and made to conform to their no-nonsense **realism**. Better have one of their own company represent moon than leave the matter up to that fleeting, shifting natural phenomenon. Of course, with the transformation of Bottom himself, this world partakes of the hlay's general confusion of reality and illusion. But Bottom is able to resolve this into a genuine union.

We gain entrance to yet a third world in this play. The fairy kingdom, presided over by Oberon and Titania, is Shakespeare's own creation. His fairies differ from those of folk tradition with respect to size, nature and activity. They are small, benevolent, and associated with flowers. Oberon and Titania speak poetry of great beauty. Puck's poetry is remarkable for rough vigor and a rustic flavor all its own. Puck, or Robin Goodfellow, is Oberon's lieutenant. His character and the poetry he speaks expressing it contrast with the delicate, airy fairies and their lyric verses. When the lovers enter the fairy world, their wooden, uninteresting speeches contrast with the flexibility and grace of speech in this other world.

Question: How are these disparate and separate worlds joined in the play?

Answer: Although the workmen and the lovers are very different indeed, connections are established between the two groups as soon as we meet the second. Later, the fairies have a great deal to do with both groups. Finally all three groups come together at the court of Duke Theseus, the lovers are married, the workmen perform, and the fairies bless the household when everyone is asleep.

When we first meet the workmen, connections between them and the lovers we have already met are established as follows: (1) The reason these men are preparing a play is to entertain at that same wedding of Theseus and Hippolyta discussed in Scene 1, at which Hermia must announce her decision; (2) The subject of the play they have chosen, while comically distant from their own world, is relevant to Hermia's plight; (3) Their plan to rehearse the next night in the Duke's wood brings them into the same geographical area as the lovers who also plan to meet there. When Oberon overhears Helena pleading for Demetrius' love, the King of Fairies decides to help and this begins his interference in the lovers' world. The fairy world and that of the lovers interweave extensively when Puck mistakes Lysander for Demetrius, with all the ensuing complications. The mischievous goblin involves the workmen in his world of moonlight and magic by placing an ass's head on Bottom. Thus transformed, this down-to-earth working man becomes the intimate companion of Titania, Queen of Fairyland. Thus the power of fairy magic affects all three worlds and this is a cohesive force in the play. It binds together the separate strands that were marked to terminate in Theseus' marriage. In short, what we have in *A Midsummer Night's Dream* is a plot structure in which the marriage of Theseus and Hippolyta is the framing event in the daylight world. It is the first thing we hear of and the last thing that happens, but the cloth that is woven within this frame is of Oberon's design. He and his assistant Puck move the shuttle of this loom madly between the straight uprights of Theseus' frame. The lovers are matched as warp and woof, and Bottom's experience runs as a strong diagonal thread knitting all sturdily.

Question: Discuss how the **theme** of change and transformation is present in this play.

Answer: There are a multitude of references to the **theme** of change and transformation, climaxing in Bottom's transformation and the change in the lovers' and Queen's eyesight. Finally a play is performed and this too concerns the **theme** under consideration, for art transforms reality. We should notice that the quarrel between Oberon and Titania is over a "changeling." It is the King's desire to have this boy which is the moving force behind the plot. Not only the cause but the result of the quarrel concerns change: Titania explains that the seasons have become all turned around as a result of the disorders in their royal household. Cause, result, and now solution concern change, for the solution of the quarrel is possible because of a change in a "little western flower" (a pansy). Furthermore, the change in the flower occurred at the same time that the Virgin Queen did not change. The arrow from Cupid's bow that was meant to change her, changed the flower instead. Finally, the power of this changed flower is to change people's eyesight so that the first creature they look upon immediately after the juice of the flower is applied is transformed into their beloved. In general, the moon, which presides over the whole play, is constantly changing from one phase to another. Both love and art look to the moon as their sovereign star, for both concern illusion and change. Art transforms reality, and we have been told over and over that love has to do not with constancy, but with change.

Question: Point out the leading motifs or images in this play and describe their occurrences.

Answer: The use of one's eyes in love is introduced right at the beginning of the play when Theseus tries to convince Hermia to obey her father. The disobedient daughter says she wishes her father saw with her eyes. The Duke replies that her eyes ought to be governed by his judgment. When Oberon steps into the picture with his love juice, we see that linking judgment to vision in matters of love is not as straightforward as Theseus thinks it is. When Helena speaks of how the blind, winged boy, Cupid, is the appropriate governor of love, she too brings up the question of using one's eyes in love. This motif comes to a **climax** when Oberon and Puck apply the magic juice to Titania, Lysander and Demetrius. The charm is specifically directed at the eyes and under its spell a person looks and loves instantly. Judgment, reason, will are all of no account whatsoever.

When the addled males protest that judgment, reason and will form the basis of their love, comedy is the result. After awakening from their enchanted experiences, Bottom and the lovers speak of what has happened in terms of eyesight. Demetrius says it's like trying to distinguish a landscape at a very great distance; Hermia feels as though he's seeing double; Helena can't believe this. Bottom speaks of having had a "most rare vision," which is a term most closely related to eyes. However, he properly widens it to include all the senses and says his vision passes beyond the evidence of all the senses. Flowers enter into the scene of this play in profusion. The fairy world that Shakespeare has created in this play is characterized in part by its association with flowers. In the scene where we first meet the fairies, nine flowers are mentioned. They continue to be mentioned throughout, and of course the love-charm is effected by use of the juice of a flower. The Duke's famous speech about "single blessedness" uses a flower to dramatize the argument.

The moon is a real presence in this play. It is mentioned many, many times and its light bathes the action of the play. At the very beginning of the play it is used by the Duke and his intended bride to measure the time until their wedding. Then the lovers make plans to meet by moonlight and elope. The workmen also plan to meet by moonlight in order to rehearse their play in privacy. The moon is important to this latter group in the further respect that they must have it in their play. Down-to-earth as they are, they have one of their own company represent Moonshine rather than leave the matter up to that shifting, fleeting celestial body. In short, the moon is sovereign of the night and it is "night-rule" that wreaks havoc in the woods.

Question: Discuss the character of Bottom the weaver.

Answer: Nick Bottom the weaver is one of Shakespeare's most memorable creations. When we first meet him, the play "Pyramus and Thisbe" is being cast. Bottom is ready to take on anything. He has complete confidence in his ability to sweep from one end of the emotional scale to the other. The energy and enthusiasm with which he participates in life are immediately evident. Some critics have objected to what they consider his domineering, brash, self-centered personality, but this is a gross misunderstanding. When he shares Titania's bower, his easy graciousness with his extraordinary new companions is a mark of his marvelous ability to adapt immediately to whatever life offers him. His energetic love of life, his naiveté and eager innocence obtain his entrance into this other-world so different from his own. And he enjoys it to the fullest. When Bottom awakens from his "dream," his own manner of reacting to it is the best approach to the experience. Wonder, awe, and a strong sense of the power beyond man's apprehension are communicated by his words there. He rightly declares the unfathomability of his "dream" and feels most profoundly its power. He knows that it should be called "Bottom's Dream" for these correct reasons. Starting from his position as a rock-bottom realist, Bottom can, with the same vigor and joy he brings to whatever he does, respond to this power and believe. The fantastically transformed Bottom, the least likely candidate for the position in the world before his transformation, becomes a participator in the fairy world in the incredible role of being Titania's beloved. But we see thus that it was possible after all. Indeed it seems an absolutely necessary liaison once we see how naturally Bottom takes to it. He conducts himself with such sobriety and yet such grace, with his own good sense and yet with such enjoyment that we see he is a weaver in this deeper sense too-Bottom the weaver is supremely capable of uniting these disparate worlds. His very person embodies the union of reality and illusion, carrying as he does Puck's trick on his real, sturdy shoulders. His love of life enables him to engage in it to the fullest. The fullness of his engagement unites experiences. In this play where love and art and dreams assert their power over life, Bottom embodies the union of reality and illusion wherein lie the secret springs and mysterious force of life itself.

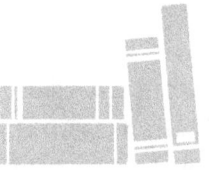

BIBLIOGRAPHY

Any paper on *A Midsummer Night's Dream* must be undertaken with a good text of the play in hand. The edition by G.L. Kittredge (Ginn, 1957) is a conservative text. The New Cambridge edition by W. A. Neilson and C. J. Hill (Houghton Mifflin, 1942) is a convenient one-volume edition of all the plays. The Arden edition by W. J. Craig and R. J. Case (Heath, 1890-1924) devotes a separate volume to each play. This edition is in the process of being replaced by the New Arden, under the general editorship of Una Ellis-Fermor, but our play has not yet appeared in the new series. A convenient text is available in paperback in the Pelican Shakespeare edited by Madeleine Doran (Penguin Books, 1959).

CRITICISM ON A MIDSUMMER NIGHT'S DREAM

Barber, Cesar Lombardi, *Shakespeare's Festive Comedy*. Princeton, 1959. An approach through social custom.

Briggs, K. M., *The Anatomy of Puck*. London, 1959. Deals with Elizabethan fairy-lore.

Brown, John Russell, *Shakespeare and His Comedies*. London, 1957. An interesting study.

Evans, Bertrand, *Shakespeare's Comedies*. New York, 1960. An example of the most current approach.

Latham, M. W., *The Elizabethan Fairies*. New York, 1930. A thorough study of Shakespeare's fairies against the background of popular and folk traditions

Schanzer, Ernest, *University of Toronto Quarterly,* xx (1951) and also xxiv (1955). An approach which offers a contrast with the others herein.

Knight, G. W., *The Shakespearean Tempest.* London, 1932. This is an interesting and stimulating study concerned with the union of image and theme.

Ransom, J. C, *Kenyon Review,* ix (1947). Deals with poetic substance of the play less extensively than the above.

EXPLORE THE ENTIRE LIBRARY OF BRIGHT NOTES STUDY GUIDES

From Shakespeare to Sinclair Lewis and from Plato to Pearl S. Buck, The Bright Notes Study Guide library spans hundreds of volumes, providing clear and comprehensive insights into the world's greatest literature. Discover more, faster with the Bright Notes Study Guide to the classics you're reading today.

See the entire library of available Bright Notes guides at **BrightNotes.com**

Available in print and digital wherever books are sold

IP INFLUENCE PUBLISHERS

www.ingramcontent.com/pod-product-compliance
Lightning Source LLC
LaVergne TN
LVHW011719060526
838200LV00051B/2953